The Journey to Find A Better You

Tricia Frances

Disclaimer: No material in this publication is intended to be a substitute for professional medical advice, diagnosis, or treatment. The author and publisher expressly disclaim responsibility for liability loss or risk incurred as a consequence, directly or indirectly, of the use and application of any of the contents of this book.

First edition published in United Kingdom by Red Road and imprint of Pennies Press 2023.
Printed by Mixam UK Ltd in the United Kingdom 2023.

Cover artwork **Secret Garden** by the author.
Typesetting by Matthew J Bird.

A CIP catalogue record of this book is available from the British Library.

ISBN 978-1-898296-15-7 (Paperback)
ISBN 978-1-898296-14-0 (Hardcover)
ISBN 978-1-898296-16-4 (e-book)

For further information about this book, please contact the author at:
https://www.triciafrances.co.uk/contact-pennies-press

This book is dedicated to all the people I have met along the way.

We cannot make it on our journey without the help sometimes of others, who like us are searching for their own truth. I would like to say a special thank you to Nuala Ronayne and Nick Hurn who were always there at the beginning when the going got tough and looked after my body when my mind was on other things. I am grateful for the wisdom and the healing. Thanks to the Spiritual Master who taught me to meditate in the Sahara Desert which led me in the direction of my **Seat** from which grew the **SECRET GARDEN**.

Thanks to all my friends over the years both here and in Spain for believing in me and to all my spirit friends for their patience!!

To Michael Heppell and my Write That Book & Word Wizards author friends for encouraging me to finally publish my book after 30 years of procrastination!

The Secret Gardeners - My Beta Readers who took the course to see if it worked on paper.

To my editors Monica Porter and Liam Todd.

To Matthew Bird (Matt) for making sure this book looks good,

And especially Cassie – my very best friend.

May the Force be ever with you!

CONTENTS
PART 1 THE WORKBOOK

CONTENTS
PART 2 THE STUDY GUIDE

CONTENTS

PART 3 THE JOURNEY

PART 1

SECRET GARDEN

THE WORKBOOK

HOW TO FIND YOUR SECRET GARDEN

Are you ready for a life-changing experience?

Sometimes we have to face the fears that we had pushed to the very far reaches of the mind, but if they need working on be sure they will rear up when you least expect them. But the beauty you find in your **Secret Garden** makes it all worthwhile, because the beauty of course is YOU.

It is a magical place within our soul which I have been developing as a life therapy through my initial meditation, piece by piece, since 1992. It is a process whereby we can look at ourselves on the deepest level and change things in our lives. We become more self-aware and aware of our bodies. It is a therapy in which we have complete control. We can obtain the keys to our kingdom through visualisation and self-analysis. I don't think we ever know everything, but with each visit to our **Secret Garden,** we become more enlightened and focused. It is extremely pioneering! How many people want to know everything about themselves and truly change? How many people want to face the fears from this and perhaps past lives? The point is, it is something that everyone can do at their own pace, whatever that is.

All types of issues can be tackled in the **Garden**, in fact, any issue that affects us as a physical or spiritual being. There are ways of eliminating trauma and negativity in our lives in a compassionate, loving way. We can learn how to recognise illness and stress and heal our bodies. If we do need help from outside we can pinpoint our specific needs and locate the type of therapy or treatment that we require. We can solve problems and puzzles. Even practical everyday needs can be met quickly and efficiently. But we must always remember that if we are asking about something that directly affects another person's path we should take into account their wishes and actions. This is about being in control of our own lives and <u>not</u> other people's.

Each person's **Secret Garden** is different, but they will have common aspects.

For example, after the initial cleansing, we look for our **Seat** which can come in many shapes and sizes. This is a starting point, where we can receive guidance, resolve problems, and watch our **Secret Garden** grow.

People ask me how long it will take to know their **Secret Garden**. I could say 'the rest of your life' but that is up to the individual and how much time they put in and if, like me, they find how much it can benefit your life. In the first instance, I would advise doing the cleansing exercises four or more times a week. It's nice to do it daily, first thing in the morning. When you know the routine add the next exercise, taking your time to know that well before moving on to the next, and so on. Once you reach your **Secret Garden** (chapter 9) my advice then is to go there three or four times a week, with other days visiting as you lay down to go to sleep, so that you can continue your journey during the night. But as I said it is up to the individual to find what suits them.

<u>So how long before I have done all the exercises in this book?</u> Well as you will see when you get to the Meditations, you don't need to do them all right away, in fact, some you might never need to do, but that will become clear as you get to that point. It would take my group participants a year of monthly workshops to learn Exercises **0-9**. By that time, their **Secret Garden** would be well established because they would have found many of the elements mentioned in the Meditations. So don't rush it. The process is ongoing and the exercises up to **9** build on each other and are the foundation of all the other meditations in the book.

An important aspect when we do this work is cleansing. We need to clean the physical, astral, and etheric bodies, so as to release negativity and therefore obtain a good connection with our **Garden**. Cold showers are a great way to clear negativity on the physical level, and/or a visualisation directly before your **Secret Garden** meditation called Cleansing.

I always teach the same technique and I have found it to work very well. You may say that you have done this before, but don't pre-judge - this is different. It is about regaining your own personal power - and the keys to your Kingdom. Sometimes you may find it will change slightly, there are no hard and fast rules but if you purposely go off the track it becomes something else. Let it flow and take you where it feels comfortable. Likewise, even after doing this work on myself for 30 years, I occasionally discover new places in my own **Secret Garden** that I have not previously seen.

Secret Garden was always taught face to face in groups – large and small. So this book was a daunting task at first as the purpose of teaching **Secret Garden** is not to 'lead' anyone, and for you to create your own **Secret Garden**, or you would just be in mine!! So I shared it with my Secret Gardeners - a lovely group of readers who gave me feedback to make sure it worked on paper.

It is important at first to follow the book as instructed. There were only 6 elements after the cleansing that I shared in my workshops and courses, the rest were found individually or as a group. Those 6 elements you will find in **Bold** in the contents list and throughout the book.

I found that if a particular meditation was not needed or it was too early then the participant would fall asleep. For example, if you try to get into the Temple before it's the right time, you just won't get in, or you will spend many meditations looking for something that is not yet there! Everything appears in your **Secret Garden** when the time is right, if you are trying to make something happen it will not flow, and you may become dissatisfied. Just go with it!

People ask me about my words stimulating their mind or their own imagination. My answer to this is 'It doesn't matter!'

If I say look for animals in your **Secret Garden** and you see a horse don't think it was your imagination, it was meant to be there - you could have just as easily thought of a cat or a zebra!!

Everything in your **Secret Garden** has a purpose; you just have to know how to recognise the signs. Don't think that you will know it all after just a few weeks. It takes years. I only started to teach the technique after I had been working with it myself for 3 years. Before we can teach we have to learn, and with **Secret Garden,** we have to learn more about ourselves first.

I hope you will enjoy the journey you are about to embark on. Make no mistake, the hardest thing in life is to really see ourselves for who we are, but it is also the most rewarding thing you will ever do - and after a while, like me, you won't be able to stop yourself from turning the page to see what comes next!

Bon voyage!

JOURNEY OBJECTIVE - **To acquire a greater understanding of yourself.**

PACKING LIST

There are a few things you need for your journey.

1) A notebook for your Journal
2) Pen, pencil and wax crayons or pencils in lots of colours
3) A quiet space to meditate.
4) An open mind!

WARNING

When we take responsibility for our own actions and our lives things change – and sometimes other people see those changes in us, and they also change. **Secret Garden** may intensify those changes. Be sure you want this shift in your life before embarking on this journey.

Secret Garden does not replace any medical procedures or treatments. Please refer to your medical team if you are unsure whether to go ahead with this technique.

You are ultimately in charge!

INTRODUCTION

The Awakening

It is a time of change.
We will finally be finding out who we are.

What is the Awakening, Enlightenment, Sacred Space, Inner Child, and **Secret Garden**?

This book aims to expand your knowledge not only of these concepts but of the self. Contained in these pages are explanations, experiences, and exercises to lead you to a better understanding of who you are.

The Awakening can be many different things to different people on a physical, mental, or spiritual level. It is a self-realisation experience. You may find thoughts and understandings outdated, or you may gain a heightened sensitivity to those around you or a shift in your state of consciousness resulting in finding your true self.

My Awakening came to me through a Near Death Experience (NDE) after an illness. Everything in these pages comes from that experience and my meditations, which guided me to write this book 30 years ago, but I was not ready. I had to share it first. Over the years I have taught this technique to 1000's of people who have benefited from it. It led me to take counselling, psychology, and nutrition qualifications.

There are many ways to become Enlightened but **Secret Garden** gives the power back to the individual. It takes you into the Sacred Space of your being, to become in tune with the soul. You can do your work in your own time, and always have control of your own situation. I am not saying that doctors, therapists, psychologists, nutritionists, and the like have no place in this process, they are an important part of life and your well-being. But you will be able to be more in tune with your body and know what you need and then seek additional or appropriate advice.

People come to their Awakening from many directions, but all have a sense of wanting to know 'What it is all about,' or why things happen to them as they do. Some feel an urgency or hear the words 'The

Time is Now.' Some have Near Death Experiences, Accidents, breakdowns, sickness, death in the family, divorce, childbirth, redundancy, and many other triggers. It's something that makes them re-evaluate their life, which brings them to this point in time.

Everyone's experience is unique and right for them and should not be judged by others' standards. Some of us have much work to do in this life to learn the lessons that we came to accomplish.

Before I take anyone into their **Secret Garden** there are many things that can be done first so that they can get a more grounded foundation for their self-work.

I have included exercises in each section. Feel free to record these if you want to, that way you won't have to keep referring to the book as you go through each one. This can be done easily these days using the Voice recorder on your mobile phone.

You will need your notebook and pens, pencils etc as mentioned in the Packing List. There are spaces to make notes and illustrations at the end of each section, but I encourage you to keep a journal from this moment on if you do not already do so. Also, keep one by your bed to write night time messages and thoughts which may increase as you work through this book. The knowledge kept in this way is invaluable for your growth. I have done this since 1992 and looking back on the information I gained through meditation has led me to formalise this and other books.

Who knows what you may be doing in the future -so remember......

'WRITE IT DOWN!'

Chapter 1

WHO ARE WE?
HOW WE SEE OURSELVES

WEB OF LIFE

The sun glinted on the gossamer strands; a raindrop hung from a thread.
A spider hunched about to strike; the fly was filled with dread.
It had landed just for a while, but when it went to leave
Its wings, stuck fast upon the wire, got worse with every heave.
The spider sat in silence, then with moves that were so slow
It closed the gap between them, but the fly still tried to go.
It slowly climbed upon the fly, then it began to prey
Not to some powerful light above, but to its dinner plate.
Think about the ones you know, are they spiders or are they flies?
Just which one do you think you are, are you the same in other's eyes?

Who are you, a spider, or a fly? Interesting thought, ask your friends, they may see you in an entirely different light to that which you see yourself in.

Many people are both. Until we start to view ourselves from different perspectives we may not know the answer to this.

Has anyone ever called you selfish, but you cannot see what they mean?

It usually means that you will not do what they want you to do. You may be self-centred sometimes but what's wrong with that? The only things that you really own in your life are your body, mind, and spirit. So if your life is intolerable for some reason then change it.

If it's uncomfortable, shift position.

Easier said than done? Maybe but the more aware you are of what you want to achieve in this life, the easier it becomes. But there is always the little matter of 'FREE WILL' to contend with.

You may see very clearly which way you want or need to go then zap, you're up against a brick wall. Husbands, wives, children, employers, shop assistants, and bank managers. These are all part of your life, and they may have very different ideas about what you should be doing and who you are! Well, we cannot change other people without repercussions, but we can change ourselves, and through that change, others change with us of their own free will - or not!

Sometimes our changes are so drastic that people around us leave, this being the case DON'T PANIC!

The following saying comes into play here,

Let it go, and if it was yours to start with it will come back to you.

and **TRUST**.

You may let go of everything and everyone. Most came back and those that don't, you will realise, was the best thing that could have happened - it clears the junk from your life... and perhaps theirs!

In a way, we are like huge bins, accumulating bits of information, people, possessions and other essential (and non-essential) worldly things. Every now and then we have to have a clear-out and polish up our reflections. It takes a while for us to get used to this new picture but when we do we are ready to start the process again. Eventually, the only thing left in the bin are the treasures.

Our life is full of reflections. When someone is treating us badly we should ask ourselves why? Did we do that to someone else in the past? Is it because we do not have self-respect? Or is it simply showing us that we deserve better?

When we are happy and smiling we spread that to the people that we meet. Go to an exhibition or fair and observe. Look at the stands where there are lots of people. The sales staff are chatty and smiling. Look at the ones sitting behind their stands alone and miserable. How many shops have you been into where you've come out thinking, 'I'm not going in there again, they are so miserable.'

What do you see when you look in the mirror? A happy face or a sad face. What would you like to see?

STOP

DO NOT GO ANY FURTHER UNTIL YOU HAVE COMPLETED THIS EXERCISE

EXERCISE 0. Calming Breath

This is the start of all meditations.

- Sit quietly where you won't be disturbed.
- Breath in and out and listen to your breathing. Do this for a few moments and try to push all thoughts out of your head by acknowledging them and then letting them go.
- Let your breath flow deep down into your belly, without forcing it.
- Try breathing in through your nose and out through your mouth. Breathe in gently and regularly to a count of 5.
- Then let it flow out gently, counting to 5 again.
- Keep doing this for about **3 or 4 minutes**.

EXERCISE 1. Colour Me

Prepare your paper or journal, coloured crayons, or pencils.

Do **Ex 0** and when you feel relaxed think about yourself. Who you are and what you do. Think about your body, your mind and your spirit. Think about your reflection, think about your emotions. Don't feel guilty or sad about parts of your life or your body you don't like. Just about how you feel right now.

When you are ready select up to 4 coloured crayons or pencils. Draw or colour how you feel. You don't have to be Picasso or Dali. It can be a match stick person with colours around, or just colour if that is what you feel. Try not to 'make' it happen. Just be spontaneous.

Reflect on your drawing for a while. What do you think it means?

***

In a workshop situation we would now go on to translate the images, so when you are ready, turn to Chapter 1 Part 2 The Study Guide, later in the book and try to translate what your image means using colour and marks, this will help you understand the process.

This is not a critical exercise, but the first step to self-awareness.

NEXT
When you finish a chapter check the study guide to see if there was anything there relevant to your experience which might be helpful. When you are happy with this move on to Chapter 2.

Chapter 2

BODY WORK
SCANNING AND SELF-HEALING
Let the Light shine from within

We have the ability to heal our mind body and spirit of many illnesses. Some health conditions may have progressed to a point where we cannot cure but we may halt the process and deal with the pain, making our lives more comfortable.

But how can we do this amazing act without the aid of a safety net?

Through meditation, visualisation and following our inner intuition.

I must add here that on no account stop taking your medication without first discussing it with your doctor or other medical advisor and it's a good idea to let them know that you are learning to meditate to help with your pain and healing.

Remember **Secret Garden** does the work at your own pace. You are not being guided by your therapist, but by the speed you turn over the pages of this book. Let the book and your inner knowing become your own private Counsellor, holistic doctor or whatever else you need right now.

If your body tells you that you need some help in certain areas then look for the therapist that can help you the most. There are guidelines later in this chapter.

But how does our body tell us we need help?

Through a process called body scanning.

As we scan our bodies we become aware of tension, strain, and where there are blockages. We can do this to ourselves and to others. When we scan another person's body we should first ask them if they mind. If this is not possible to ask them we silently ask their higher self by simply saying 'is it OK to scan your body.' If it isn't you won't be able to do it!! Our body is our temple, and it is sacred. We do not have the right to enter another's Sacred Space without first requesting permission to do so.

I have had a lot of fun at seminars with public body scanning. I ask a willing volunteer to stand at the front of the room. Then I ask the audience to look at this person, starting at his feet and working their way up his body with their eyes. When their eyes stop or if they think they see something they make a mental note of where it is. At the end, it is surprising how many people actually find the places where the volunteer has a problem.

At one event we had a young man in front of an audience of 40 people. He felt he was perfectly healthy until we picked up half a dozen or so points. We told him what we'd seen, and he said he felt he was quite healthy and didn't relate to most of it. But his mother was in the audience, and she said that we were right on all counts - most of his problems came, as I suspected, from when he was a small child!!

So why can we still pick these things up 30 or more years later? Mostly it is because they have never been cleared from the aura.

Many things that happen to our physical body come from outside it in the first instance. Take the example of stress. We argue with a loved one, or we go for an important interview. We feel the tension in our stomach area. This is the Solar Plexus, our emotional centre (more about this in the Chakra chapter).

It can initially lead to an upset stomach and headaches. With prolonged stress in this area over a period of time, it can lead to more serious illness. If we look at illness it isn't difficult to see where it comes from. We need to find the root cause before we can find a cure, otherwise we are only skimming the surface all the time. If you would like to explore this further see Louise Hay's book 'Heal Your Body.' It lists many ailments, reasons for them and affirmations.

So how do we clear things from our aura, and how do we know what it is and what has caused it?

It is possible to use meditation and visualisation to increase the healing process, as a means of self-discovery, to become spiritually enlightened, to address pressing problems and fears and to relieve stress, illness, and pain in the physical body, so leaving us feeling more satisfied and healthier.

Whilst doing the following exercise we will often become aware of where or when the problem first arose. It can cause a sudden outburst of tears or laughter, let it go - it is all part of the process.

EXERCISE 2 Body Scan

Sit or lay in a comfortable position, relax, and listen to your breathing as in **Ex 0**.

PART 1

Starting at the tip of your toes tense your muscles to a count of 5 and release. First your toes, then your feet, ankles, calves, knees, up and up till you get to your shoulders. Then go back to your fingers and up your arms to your shoulders again. Then neck, jaw and to your face, tensing and releasing. When you get to the top of your head imagine any tension left in your body blowing out of a little hole on the top of your head - your crown chakra.

Lay still enjoying this new state of relaxation that you have acquired at your own pace, all by yourself.

PART 2

When you are totally relaxed visualise a wall of golden light at your feet. It looks solid but as you watch it you will see it begin to move very slowly – think of the scanner on a photocopier or your printer.

As the light scans your body it will pick up any blocks you have. When this happens it will seem to get stuck. When the light comes to a block fill that area with more gold light. If it fails to move then follow the gold light with white healing lasers, blasting the negativity that is causing the blockages. When the golden scanner moves again allow it to glide gently along your body towards your head, clearing and healing as it goes. When it reaches the head allow any negativity that is left to be released through the crown as before. Enjoy the experience, knowing that your physical body is being healed with love and when you are ready slowly come back into the room. Knowing you can repeat this healing meditation again tomorrow or when you next feel the need.

It is not uncommon to experience such things as touching, manipulation, visions etc. whilst doing this exercise. This is part of the healing process. If it has been a major healing, please treat it as you would any other type of treatment, with respect and take it easy. You won't want to undo what you have just lovingly spent time doing.

Depending on your ailment it is recommended that you repeat this exercise daily or at least once or twice a week.

WHICH THERAPY

You may be able to do this work yourself but if you need help use this list as a guide for the following problems (not forgetting your GP, Physiotherapist, or medical advisor.) There are many more options than on this list, but it will start you thinking of where to get help.

Later in your meditations, you can ask for help for a specific condition and the answers may come there.

BACK & NECK	Reflexology, Acupuncture, Osteopathy, Aromatherapy, Kinesiology.
CIRCULATION	Massage, Reflexology, Aromatherapy, Acupuncture
OVERWEIGHT	Dietician, Nutritionist, Reflexology, Counselling, Personal Trainer
MIND & EMOTIONS	Counselling, Aromatherapy, Flower Remedies
SPIRIT	Spiritual Teachers & Counsellors, Vibrational medicine, Healer
PHOBIAS	Past life therapy, Counselling, Shamanic Rebirthing
ARTHRITIS	Dietician, Aromatherapy, Reflexology, Acupuncture, Nutritionist.
ALLERGIES	Nutritionist, Kinesiology

NEXT

When you finish a chapter check the study guide to see if there was anything there relevant to your experience which might be helpful. When you are happy with this move on to Chapter 3.

Chapters 3 & 4
Gaining the Keys to the Kingdom
The Cleansing & The Waterfall

Arise my spirit and Awake my soul,
Free me from barriers and let me give my all.
I'll be in tune with myself and then I'll find,
An awakening for body spirit and mind.

To be relaxed is essential not only for Meditation but for Life itself. Many methods exist but there is a specific method used for **SECRET GARDEN** work.

We have the ability here to find out who we really are, and by being in touch with our **Secret Garden** we can make our lives more enjoyable and healthier. We can resolve problems, change the energy around events, become empowered and find the way to our soul.

As we become more aware we look for something just out of our reach, a feeling that something is missing. By finding our **Secret Garden** we will be able to answer questions, meet our **Guides** (helpers in our **Secret Garden**) and resolve problems that previously seemed unresolvable, on a soul level. We will see ourselves for what we really are and know that the reflections are truly us.

We can change everything in our life; past, now and future. Perhaps not the actual event but the energy around it, by doing this we start to clear * Karma, and get rid of baggage, then we can move into a more healthy, positive future.

The Keys to your Kingdom are gained through self-reflection and visualisation. They lead you to parts of yourself that you may not even know exists. Each time you go into your **Secret Garden** you will help it to grow and discover more 'Keys.'

But before you can find your way into your **Secret Garden** you have one more cleansing to do. This opens the way for you to move forward.

* **AUTHOR NOTE.** KARMA – we will get to this later, but a simple explanation is 'Karma is the consequences of our actions.'

Chapter 3

The CLEANSING

Before going into the **Secret Garden** we have to release the negativity that surrounds us in our everyday life. This is the Essential first step. To go into the **Secret Garden** without cleansing leads to being too cluttered with everyday experiences. We need to try to get rid of them before we can start work.

I call this tuning in. It always follows the same process and if done every day, especially first thing in the morning, you will be more aware and ready for anything as the day unfolds.

* Ideally the meditation should follow a cold shower. It clears negativity that may be around you, stimulates the system and gives a general feeling of well-being. But like any physical activity, if you are worried about your health you should seek advice before embarking on anything which is a shock to the system.

In the first part of the meditation you will be filled with light which cleanses the aura, then in Chapter 4, you will be taken into the **Waterfall** to cleanse the etheric body.

*** AUTHORS NOTE**

There is an alternative to the cold shower!!

A cold shower is not always a practical step for everyone – so you can use the following Cleansing **Ex 3** and **Waterfall Ex 4** Meditations instead.

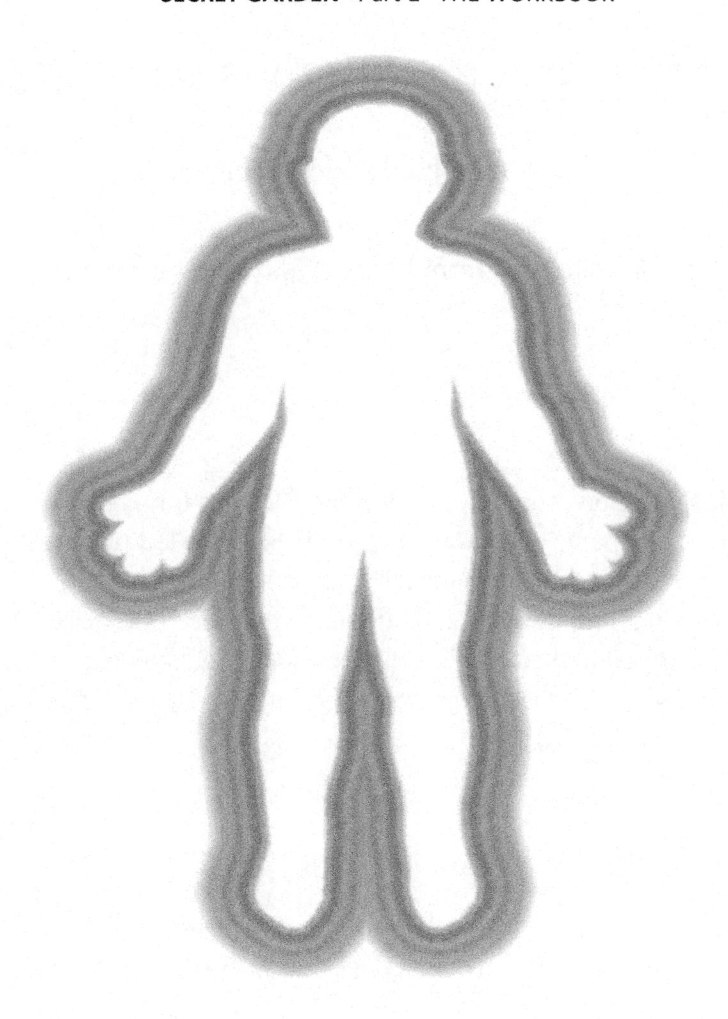

WHAT IS THE AURA?

The Aura – or subtle body - can be described as the energy field that surrounds the human body or any other living being – e.g. animals, trees, plants etc. It could also surround inanimate objects, but those auras are not so easily detected. The layers are represented by the colours of the Chakras (see Chapter 20). The Etheric Body is the closest part of the Aura to our physical body. Enough to know right now that we have an energy field that surrounds the body. You will be able to find out how to see an aura when you turn to the Study Guide after you have completed this chapter.

EXERCISE 3. CLEANSING VISUALISATION

(This can be recorded) (**5-10 minutes**)

This is the start to all your Meditations from here on and incorporates Ex 0.

Get comfortable and close your eyes.

Take a few deep breaths and still your mind.

- Sit quietly where you won't be disturbed.
- Breath in and out slowly and listen to your breathing. Do this for a few moments and try to clear all thoughts from your mind by acknowledging them and then letting them go.
- Let your breath flow deep down into your belly, without forcing it.
- Now as you breathe in gently and regularly through your nose, the breath comes up your back from the soles of your feet to the top of your head. Hold it to a count of 5.
- Then as you breathe out through your mouth the breath flows gently down your front to the soles of your feet counting to 5 again.

Do this for a few minutes until you feel calm.

- Now see yourself standing in a void, and from above a golden ray is shining down. It shines through the top of your head; this is your crown chakra. The golden ray flows through your body filling it with light.
- See the light shine through your chakra centres into the aura around your body, cleansing it.
- If there are any dark spaces fill them with a starburst or golden light which will take away any dark negative areas.

Do this for a few minutes.

- When your aura is clear and full of golden light try to extend it out as far as possible.
- When you feel it is as large as you can make it and your aura is clean and bright, bring the golden light back inside, leaving all negativity far outside your body.
- You will be standing in a golden clean space around your body, which is your aura.
- If you are only doing the cleansing meditation and want to exit take some deep breaths, bring the light back inside you, hold for a few moments then open your eyes.
- Take a few moments to notice how you feel after this experience.

This is the complete **Cleansing** which is the best way to begin each time you sit down to meditate. It can take some time to get used to doing this process, but it will come naturally after a while. You are now ready to continue with all of the **Secret Garden** Meditations.

NEXT

When you finish this Exercise turn to the Study Guide Chapter 3 to learn how to see auras and anything else that is relevant to this experience. Then move on to Chapter 4.

Chapter 4

The Waterfall

Meditation helps to align our mind body and spirit, which in turn enhances our lives, making us happier, healthier, and more fulfilled.

At the same time, it makes us more aware of our surroundings, other people, and the planet we live on. We are tenants here on Earth, doing the best we can whilst we are here. But we could do more, and by being in tune with our mind, body, and spirit we can work on multi-dimensions, instead of just in the physical.

<u>Let's Recap</u>: **The routine for entering your Garden uses Exercise 3 in Chapter 3 (which incorporates Ex 0). This is the start to all your meditations from this point until Exercise 5.**

So by now, we know how to prepare to enter the **Waterfall.** This is at the entrance to your **Cave**, which you will find in Chapter 5. From there you will be able to access your **Secret Garden**.

EXERCISE 4. The WATERFALL

(This can be recorded)

Continue from **Ex 3**.

- ♥ Walk forwards a few paces and you will see a **Waterfall** which is like sparkling rain or tiny lights.
- ♥ Stand under it allowing the water to wash over you to cleanse your etheric body which directly surrounds your physical body.
- ♥ See yourself glowing from the water or lights that are washing over you.
- ♥ When you feel light or sparkling or surrounded by bright light it's time to leave the **Waterfall**.
- ♥ If you want to exit your meditation now take some deep breaths, bring the light back inside you, hold for a few moments then open your eyes.

Before we move on reflect on how that made you feel. Write it down.

You have done a lot of work so far. If you have never meditated before you will now have the basics for any meditation.

NEXT

When you finish Chapters 3 & 4 turn to the Study Guide to see if there is anything there that is relevant to your experience which might answer your questions. When you are happy with this move on to Chapter 5.

Chapters 5 & 6

The Cave & The Pool

Safe Sacred Space

After meditation, we are very open. This means that we are vulnerable to pick up negative energies either from other people or from energies around us. So we have to close down. This can be done in many ways but here are three simple ways for beginners. You could do these at any time, you don't have to be in a meditation, but it is a good idea to do it each time you exit the **Waterfall** and your meditation. It also has a way of grounding you, as some meditations can leave you a bit light-headed.

PROTECTION VISUALISATIONS

TECHNIQUE 1

See a spiral of gold light starting at your feet and winding itself around you up past the top of your head. It is in your aura and so does not restrict your movements. Visualise

TECHNIQUE 2

You are a rose or another flower of your choice. You are in full bloom but as you watch, your petals begin to close until they are a tight bud. Visualise

TECHNIQUE 3

You Visualise pulling a large cloak of light around you until you are completely covered. The cloak is impenetrable, but you can see through. Wear the cloak in any threatening or uncomfortable situation to relieve the feelings of stress and make you feel more comfortable and at the end of a meditation. (Think of the Invisibility cloak in Harry Potter books!)

By now you have learnt the basics for **Secret Garden** meditations and have mastered **Ex 3** in your own way and have experienced the **Waterfall** which leads to your **Cave**. So, now your adventure begins.

First, it's time to find the entrance to the **Secret Garden** and create a safe place.

The entrance is in the Cave and the safe space is in the Pool. So off we go.......

Chapter 5

The Cave

The **Cave** is the entrance into your **Secret Garden** and is at the beginning of all meditations after Cleansing and the **Waterfall**.

EXERCISE 5. The CAVE

(This can be recorded)

Continue from **Ex 3 & 4**.

- As you walk out of the **Waterfall** feeling cleansed and refreshed you will find yourself at the entrance of a **Cave.** Before moving forward any further stand at the entrance and look around you. Somewhere in the **Cave** is a **Pool** of water, we will get to that later.
- What else can you see?
- What are you walking on and what is above you?
- It's time to explore your **Cave** for around **10 – 15 minutes**.
- When you are ready to leave walk towards the entrance of your **Cave** but before you exit, look to see if there is something there for you. If so pick it up. This is your first gift from your **Secret Garden.** Take it with you when you walk back through the **Waterfall** and into your room having brought the light back inside you as you exit.
- Take a few breaths and write in your notebook what you found and saw in your **Cave.**

I don't want to influence you whilst exploring your **Cave** so check the Study Guide after your meditation which may give you some answers.

You may often find a gift at the entrance to your **Cave**. Usually when you leave but sometimes there might be something there as you enter, this will be of use to you in your meditation, either in the **Cave** or the **Secret Garden** or for when you exit.

What did you see? What were the walls like? Was it dark or light? How did you feel?

Did you go anywhere else? Were there any colours?

NEXT

When you are happy with this, move on to Chapter 6 The **Pool** or turn to the Study Guide to see if there is anything there that is relevant to your experience which might answer your questions in Chapter 5.

Chapter 6

The Pool

The **Pool** is your safe place. It is a **Pool** of Healing. It's where you can relax and be healed. If there is ever anything in your **Secret Garden** or **Cave** that you do not want there then it can be thrown into the **Pool** where it will transmute to positive energy and be released from your **Cave**. It won't return to your **Garden** or your **Pool**.

EXERCISE 6. The POOL

(This can be recorded)

Continue from **Ex 5**

- When you are ready walk through the **Waterfall** into the **Cave** behind it. You will see a **Pool**; it can take any form. This is the **Pool** of healing. Remember. If you ever see anything in your **Cave** or **Secret Garden** that you are uncomfortable with and you want to get rid of, throw it into the **Pool** where it will transmute into positive energy and disappear.
- Step towards the **Pool** and if you want to, jump in, and feel the water healing and comforting you. If you are feeling unwell or stressed this is where you can relax and feel relief from your problem letting the water wash your troubles away.
- Take some time to sit in or by your **Pool** feeling the relaxing sound or look of the water.
- Look about. What can you see from this position?
- When you are ready exit the **Pool** area and walk towards the entrance of your **Cave** but before you exit, look by the entrance to see if there is another gift for you. If so pick it up and take it with you. Your gift this time might not have been a physical object, but it may have been spending the time to relax at your **Pool**.

- Walk back through the **Waterfall** and into your room having brought the light back inside you as you exit the **Waterfall**.
- Take a few breaths and write in your notebook what you experienced in your **Pool**.

Meditation time guide **Ex 3-5 + 5-10 mins**

Did you find the **Pool**, and did you get into it? You will now be able to bathe in the **Pool** any time you wish. It is here that the healing process begins.

OK, it's finally time to get into your Garden!

But to get into it you first have to find the crack or opening in the wall of the **Cave**, that is the way into your **Secret Garden**, but you might not always get in!

Don't worry, that's normal – it still happens to me on occasion. There is always a reason for it. Your **Cave** is the inner you, it's where your emotions are stored, where you can look in depth at yourself. There is much more to the **Cave** than there first appears to be – that's why you will find the **Pool** there, the place to dissolve those negative thoughts and actions.

Look about the **Cave** and see what's happening. Do you need to spend more time in the **Pool** or is there another task you need to be doing before you can leave the **Cave** and enter your **Secret Garden**?

You will learn how to find the crack in the wall in the next chapter.

NEXT

When you finish Chapters 5 & 6 turn to the Study Guide to see if there is anything there that is relevant to your experience which might answer your questions. When you are happy with this move on to Chapter 7.

Chapters 7 & 8

Entering the Secret Garden
The Seat & The Garden

As we become more aware we look for something just out of our reach, a feeling that something is missing. By finding our **SECRET GARDEN** *we will be able to answer questions, meet our* **Guides** *and resolve problems on a soul level, that previously seemed unresolvable. With the help of this book, we can travel back to our childhood and face our inner child, acknowledging our dreams, and find our true self.*

Most meditations take around 10-20 minutes including the Exercises 3-5. But at the beginning or if there is a lot to do, it could take longer 30-40 minutes. You really don't want to be meditating for hours on end – you have a life outside your **Secret Garden**! You should come back into your room naturally, but I have seen during my meditation groups that some people need a bit of a nudge (speaking their name softly until they are back). So if you find this is you and hours are spent during your day meditating make a note of the time when you start and set a gentle phone timer for your preferred exit time e.g. 30 minutes.

Chapter 7

The Seat

This is where it all begins. The **Seat** is really the first stop in the **Garden**. It is a very important **Seat**. You can resolve any problem here. It is a meeting place too where you can get help from your **Guides**. It is essential that this is found before going on as without our **Seat** we often do not find where we are going. When we first come into the **Garden** after washing our etheric, auric, and physical bodies we must then clear our mind of the trauma of the day. Any problems encountered at this point in our life can be faced also. The **Seat** is the starting point, as we sit down we state what is troubling us and often we are given the answers - but beware they are not always straight forward! We may be given a page reference in a book or shown something that at first we do not understand. Take it further and the answer will clarify.

The **Seat** can be anything: a rock, a stone, a mound of grass, a tree trunk, a wooden bench, or even a throne. Do not think about what you would like it to be. Just go in there and find it!

EXERCISE 7. The SEAT

(This can be recorded)

Continue from **Ex 5**

- When you are ready to leave the **Cave** look around for a crack or gap in the wall. When you find it walk through and you will find yourself in your **Garden**. Look about for your **Seat**. It should be close by. It may be anything that you feel is right for you. This is a place where you can sit whenever you need to solve a problem.
- When you find your **Seat** sit down and look around your **Garden**.
- What does it feel like?
- What can you see? How big is your **Garden**? Do you have a good view or is it restricted in some way?
- What can you hear? Listen carefully. This is where to learn to listen to the silence which will bring balance and understanding.
- What is the weather like?
- What can you smell?
- Take some time here and if you have a problem ask for help.
- When you are ready walk back to the **Cave**. Just outside the crack, you will see something on the ground. This is a gift from the **Garden**. Pick it up and bring it with you through the crack, into the **Cave**, through the **Waterfall** and back into your room.

Meditation time guide **Ex 3-5 + 10 – 15 mins**

Chapter 8

THE SECRET GARDEN

We have finally arrived at our destination. But this is just the beginning!

In your **Secret Garden** are many things and each time you go in you will see it grow.

Explore places you haven't been before, until you begin to know where everything is – and then it will keep on growing, so you have new places to experience. It does not have to be a traditional **Garden**. It can be a **Garden** you know or something completely new. Go with it, do not try to manipulate it into something that you understand. It will become clear.

There are many things to discover in your **Garden**, and many adventures to be had, whilst finding yourself. So fasten your safety belts and in we go!!

EXERCISE 8. The GARDEN

(This can be recorded)

Continue from **Ex 5**

- When you are ready, leave the **Cave** through the crack in the wall. Walk away from this entrance into your **Garden** and sit on your **Seat**.
- Look around – what can you see?
- Can you see or hear water? It can be a river or a pond, or maybe even the sea.
- What else do you see?
- Are there flowers or trees?
- What is the weather like?
- Are there any animals?
- You may find that there seems to be a fence or some sort of perimeter around your **Garden.** Do not worry, this is just the boundaries of your mind, this will expand the more you go to your **Secret Garden.**
- If you feel up for it get up from your **Seat** and walk around. Don't go too far just yet, you want to know every inch of your **Garden** so that you can remember what it looks like all the time.
- Enjoy yourself exploring.
- When you are ready make your way back to the **Waterfall**. Walk through, bring the light back inside you and come back into your room.

Meditation time guide **Ex 3-5 + 15-20 mins**

EXERCISE 8b. Colour My Secret Garden

Do you remember the Colour Me picture you made in Exercise 1?

Now that you have the basic keys to enter your **Secret Garden**, the gateway to your soul, it's time to draw your first image of your **Secret Garden**.

After the meditation, please get your coloured crayons, pens or pencils and paper ready.

Like before you don't have to be Picasso or Dali. This is for your reference.

Remember that you have control in your **Garden**. It can be however you wish. Often it will grow in a completely unexpected way. At a later date, it is good to draw it again to see how it has grown.

So you might choose to draw a map or floor plan, or a more pictorial illustration – or a mix of both.

Try not to 'make' it happen. Just be spontaneous. Try to capture the things you saw or make a list if you can't remember where they were.

Reflect on your drawing for a while. What do you think of your **Garden**?

***

NEXT

When you finish Chapters 7 & 8 turn to the Study Guide to see if there is anything there that is relevant to your experience which might answer your questions. When you are happy with this move on to Chapter 9.

Chapter 9

THE GUIDES

Our **Guides** are people or creatures in our **Garden** that help us to learn about ourselves, and to help us to resolve our issues. This is the last piece of the basic **Secret Garden** technique. You now have all the tools you need to embark on your Journey of Discovery to find YOU.

Extension of **Ex 7 The Seat**

- ♥ Take your place on your **Seat**.
- ♥ It's time to meet your first Guide – it could be in animal or human form.
- ♥ Is there anyone there with you by your **Seat**? Or in your **Garden**?
- ♥ If you have any problems at the moment you can ask for help to resolve these.
- ♥ If they don't immediately appear, glance around you. Or close your eyes and send out a message about something you need help with.
- ♥ They may appear with a message for you or answer your request for help. Or they may just be there – silently supporting.
- ♥ They may want to take you further into the **Garden**. If so walk with them for a while and ask them questions as this is the way you learn.
- ♥ Never be afraid of anything in your **Garden**, if there is something you do not like, remember you can take it back to the **Pool** of healing in the **Cave**, where it will be transmuted into positive energy.
- ♥ Enjoy this new experience and when you are ready, make your way back to your **Seat** or the **Cave**.
- ♥ Pick up anything left there for you, walk back through the **Waterfall** and into your room.

NEXT. Reflect on what you found and write your notes. When you finish Chapter 9 turn to the Study Guide to see if there is anything there that is relevant to your experience which might answer your questions. When you are happy with this move on to Section 2 The Meditations.

SECTION 2 THE MEDITATIONS

Seeing Our Garden Grow

From here on you can do the Meditations in any order you choose.
Meditation time guide for the following exercises is Ex 3-5 + 10 – 20 mins.

You have done well to get to this point in such a short time. It would usually take a year of monthly workshops to get here. Some of the following guided meditations are very specific which may not be right for you at this time, so skip those for now. With **Secret Garden,** you are always in control.

When leading workshops I only gave 6 elements, shown in bold throughout: **Waterfall, Cave, Pool, Seat, Garden, and Guides.** You have now had access to all.

Everything else was found by those meditating in the groups. There has to be more in this book because you don't have access to me or my groups, so you will find other elements from now on. And from here on you could move into the next chapter if you cannot get into the one you are reading.

Something that I have found over the years is that if a person is not ready for a meditation they will miss that workshop or fall asleep. If this happens to you, don't worry, just continue to work on the previous meditations and **Ex 3-5** a bit longer, then try again, or try another Meditation from this section.

That's why the Study guide is so useful. It will explain some of the things that you might find. But going forward it's best to continue with the Workbook before reading the corresponding chapter in the Study Guide so that you are not influenced by the information there.

You want it to be your own **Secret Garden**, so it is important to do one chapter in the Workbook and then the Study guide at a time. But from now you can pick and choose your Meditations and do them in any order you wish. E.g. if you need to let go of people or things in your life, do the Hot Air Balloon meditation and so on.

You may find now that you are in a deep meditative state and may feel giddy on your return So remember to come back slowly: have a last look around your **Garden**, make your way back to the **Cave** then the **Waterfall**, look at or pick up any gifts you find at the entrance and then walk back into your room, taking a few deep breathes and bringing the light back inside you before opening your eyes, knowing that you can return to your **Secret Garden** any time you like.

DON'T FORGET! If there is ever anything in your **Garden** that you don't want there just take it back to the **Cave** and throw it into the **Pool** where it will transmute to positive energy.

REMEMBER

The following Meditations are interactive and can be taken in any order. All are ongoing.

Don't forget how to make an Exit!

If you want to exit your meditation before moving on to the next one, find your way back to the Waterfall, and as you leave it bring the light back inside, take some deep breaths, hold for a few moments then open your eyes and you will be back in your room.

It's best to finish a meditation with this for exiting otherwise you may feel disorientated.

Chapter 10

MEDITATION
THE CRYSTAL
Transformation - Facets of the Self

The Crystal represents you. All the facets of your personality, your thoughts, your mind, your Ego, your body – your Self.

Do you know that **YOU** are the most important person? Without you no one else has you.

Extension of **Ex 5 The Cave**

- Look around your **Cave**. Somewhere you will see a huge crystal. It might be by your **Pool**, or it could be further back.
- Walk around the Crystal, looking for any dull areas.
- Select the area that you are drawn to and feel where it is in your Self.
- Look about for something to polish or clean that facet with.
- Think about how it feels once you have cared for it and cleaned it.

Spend some time by it, it is all the parts of You. When you are ready walk back to the **Waterfall** and back into your room.

Chapter 11

MEDITATION
THE HOT AIR BALLOON
Freedom

We often allow people and situations to hold us back in our lives. We can free ourselves from that by cutting the ties that bind us. Once we are free from those constricting ties, those that are meant to be in our lives will come back.

Extension of **Ex 8 The Garden**

- ♥ Look around your **Garden**. Somewhere you will see a Hot Air Balloon.
- ♥ It could be close by or far away. Walk to it and look around it.
- ♥ Find out how is it being held down to the Earth.
- ♥ See how thick the ropes or wires are that bind it down.
- ♥ Climb into the basket and look about for something to cut these binds with.
- ♥ As you cut through each of them, visualise who or what that is that is holding you down. Some may be difficult to cut.
- ♥ When the final one is cut through you see yourself rising high above.
- ♥ You will be free from people or situations that have held you back.
- ♥ When you are ready visualise yourself back in your **Garden**, your **Cave**, or the **Waterfall**.
- ♥ Come back into your room.

Chapter 12

MEDITATION
THE TEMPLE OF KNOWLEDGE
AKASHIC RECORDS

This is the Living Library. The ever changing books of our lives. It's the place to find out why we are here. Where we can look back and perhaps forward. It holds all the books of all the people that have lived. Your book is there. This is the only book that you will be able to read. You may not find it for some time. Keep checking as it will appear when you are ready.

Extension of **Ex 8 The Garden**

- ♥ Somewhere in your **Garden** in the distance there is a large building. This is the Temple of Knowledge.
- ♥ Look around your **Garden**, can you see it? When you do see it, try to get to it.
- ♥ Your journey there may be easy or there could be obstacles.
- ♥ When you are there go inside. It is full of books for as far as you can see. Look around and then go and find a **Seat** somewhere inside where the sun is shining through.
- ♥ Now go to one of the shelves and take down a book that you are drawn to. Take it back to that **Seat** and sit and hold it in your hands, looking at the cover, the title, and the size.
- ♥ Open it up and read what it says inside. This is your book.
- ♥ When you have read what you need to know put the book away for now. You can come back and look at it any time.
- ♥ Go outside, close the door and walk back towards your **Garden Seat**.
- ♥ Reflect on what you have seen for a while.
- ♥ When you are ready walk back to your **Cave**, through the **Waterfall** and into your room.

Chapter 13

MEDITATION
THE GIVING TREE
Abundance

Abundance is to have more than you need and comes in many forms. It is not always about financial gain. It can be the love of friends and family, the feeling of goodwill when you have been able to help someone, or they have helped you, it can be receiving a gift or being able to share with others .

Extension of **Ex 8 The Garden**

- ♥ In your **Garden** there is a Tree of Abundance. Go and look around until you find it.
- ♥ Now sit or stand under your tree and relax, focusing on what you have or what you need in your life.
- ♥ Often it will fall from the tree, or when you look up you will see it or a symbol of some kind hanging in the branches.
- ♥ If it is symbolic, work out what that means to you.
- ♥ Things are not always straight forward in your **Garden**.
- ♥ When you are ready, take your gift of Abundance and leave your **Garden** or sit on your **Seat** and ask for help to translate your gift.
- ♥ When you are ready leave your **Garden** and **Cave** through your **Waterfall** and back into your room.

Chapter 14

MEDITATION
HEART LIGHT & TEMPLE OF LOVE
Healing Love

Sometimes we have to deal with emotion ties with family, friends, or other people. Sometimes there are issues to be worked out and other times we might just want to show our love to those close to us. We cannot change what has happened in the past, but we can change the energy around situations and within ourselves and the way we think about it.

Extension of **Ex 5 & 6 The Pool in the Cave**

Healing Relationships – **Heart Light**

- Stand by your **Pool** in the **Cave**, it is your **Pool** of Healing. Think of up to 3 people that you want to work with there. Sometimes at the start it is easier to work with one at a time.
- Visualise them standing facing you and imagine that you have a veil over your heart chakra.
- Raise the veil and send a beam of love in the form of light towards the heart of the other person for around 5 seconds. Do this 3 times then close the veil to protect your heart.
- Sometimes that person will not stand still. It can take up to 3 months to do this work daily on each person. Persevere as it's a wonderful thing when they align with you, and you can touch palms or hug with no difficulty.
- If it becomes too difficult or too uncomfortable, put them into your **Pool** or send them out of your **Cave**.
- If you have more than one person waiting for your heart light by the **Pool**, now is the time to work with the second person, then the third.
- One at a time place each person in the **Pool** as you finish the healing with your heart light, they will disappear either by transmuting to positive energy or in a way that you visualise, so that your **Cave** is private to you again. Then either step into the **Pool** of healing and sit for a while or leave your **Cave** through the **Waterfall**.

Extension of **Ex 5 & 6 The Pool in the Cave or 8 The Garden**

Healing Situations – **Temple of Love**

I have set this either in your **Garden** or by your **Pool** in your **Cave**. You may find your Temple of Love, but this does not always appear as you may think. It can be a building in the **Garden**, a tree, a movie screen, or it could be a section of your own **Cave**.

Working in a similar way to Healing Relationships Meditation send your Healing Love to a situation or event that you would like to change.

- ♥ Stand by your **Pool** of Healing or go into the **Garden** and find your Temple of Love.
- ♥ When you have found a suitable location, think of a situation from the past that you want to change. It may be a reaction to something that happened, or it may be the people involved that you want to work on. You can't change the past. But you can change the way you feel about it.
- ♥ Work on just one event at a time. It could take up to 3 months working daily on it before it is resolved within you. This often also leads to changes in the people involved - because you have changed.
- ♥ Visualise the event and surround it with healing light.
- ♥ Have conversations with yourself and perhaps those people that were involved, remembering why it happened.
- ♥ Now view that situation again, this time looking at it from all angles. Could you have avoided it. Would the outcome have been the same if you had reacted differently. Visualise how you would have preferred the outcome. Could you have made that happen?
- ♥ If you had little or no control over the situation, visualise how it has made you stronger and good things that have come or will come from that event.
- ♥ Now think about how much more positive your life will be when you let it go.
- ♥ Now step into your **Pool** of healing and clear any negativity that might have come up through this exercise.
- ♥ Know that this is your life, and you have control on how you view it.
- ♥ When you are ready leave your **Garden** or **Cave** then through the **Waterfall**.

Chapter 15

MEDITATION
THE INNER SANCTUARY
Deep inside the Cave - TRUE YOU

Somewhere in your **Cave** there is a hidden room or space. Here you can work on the deepest level on things hidden away even from your Self. Work here is not always easy and if you find it too difficult leave and come back another time when you are ready.

Extension of **Ex 5 The Cave**

- ♥ Look around your **Cave** for a place that you have not noticed before, or that you have avoided.
- ♥ Have a look at how it presents itself and when you are ready enter.
- ♥ You may want to sit or stand, explore or be still to see what comes into your mind.
- ♥ It is warm and comfortable here. It is where you can really be in touch with your deeper and higher self. It is where you can re-programme your life.
- ♥ If you see something that you want to change then this is the place to do it but remember that it will affect your life so be absolutely sure you want these changes.
- ♥ Think about that change and how it can be achieved. Or ask for some guidance. It might be an image making you aware of where you are in your life and clarifying that change.
- ♥ Stay for a while until you feel you have got the answer you were looking for. Don't forget – it is not always easy to understand at first.
- ♥ When you are ready to leave your inner sanctuary, enjoy a walk back to your **Seat** to relax. You have accomplished much today.
- ♥ When you are ready walk back through your **Cave** and **Waterfall** and into your room.

Chapter 16

MEDITATION
THE SACRED MOUNTAIN
Wisdom beyond limits

To get to our mountain we have to break down walls and fences, it's a long way and we may have to think beyond our limits, but we CAN make it.

Extension of **Ex 8 The Garden**

- ♥ Sit on your **Seat** and look into the distance. Do you see the mountains? It's time to go there.
- ♥ Perhaps you will be guided or maybe you will take that adventure on your own.
- ♥ You may need things for your journey, don't worry you will find them on your way.
- ♥ This journey is unique to you, and you will find what you need. It is often either about facing your fears or finding who the real you is.
- ♥ There will be help to do this.
- ♥ Often this is not a one trip experience, you may have to come back several times to complete this part of your journey.
- ♥ When you are ready make your way back to your **Cave**, through the **Waterfall** and into your room.

NOTE. There will be more clues about this adventure in the study guide and Part 3 – The Journey. Please give this a try a few times before resorting to those resources!

Chapter 17

MEDITATION
THE PATH TO THE WHITE HOUSE
Family - Our Roots

In our **Garden** just out of sight, perhaps along a Path that we have not yet seen, is a White House where we find family and the lessons we have been given by them.
It's time to finally to face those lessons.

Extension of **Ex 8 The Garden**

- Leave your **Cave** and sit on your **Seat**. Look all around. You may have been focusing in front of you previously, now look to the sides and maybe behind.
- You will see a path. Where does it lead.
- You may already see the white house, if not follow the path to find it.
- Sometimes this takes a long time, years even. Don't give up, it will appear when you are ready.
- This house is your family home. It may look different to your physical home. It's a place where you have been loved. But family is also something that is not always easy.
- When you are ready enter your house.
- Anything that you need to do there will appear at some point now or in the future.
- Remember it is safe in your **Garden**. If the work here is too difficult right now, leave and come back another time.
- Remember that you can use the Heart Light on those people either in the Temple of Love or by your **Pool** in your **Cave**.
- Go back to your **Seat** and reflect on what you found.
- When you are ready go back to your **Cave** and **Waterfall** and back into your room.

Chapter 18 & 19

MEDITATION
EXTENDING THE BOUNDARIES
Location meditations

There are two last meditations that I wanted to include that take you outside your meditation space into the real world: The River & The Woods.

When meditating outside your usual space, make sure that you are in a safe environment, with someone else or somewhere that you will not be disturbed.

These meditations can be very powerful and are often enjoyable with other people. I included at least one when running my courses.

Chapter 18

MEDITATION
THE RIVER
Reflections

Extension of **The Garden** meditation process but can be simplified as below.

- Make yourself comfortable and look about you. What can you see and hear.
- Close your eyes your and remember the way the river and surrounding area looked.
- With your eyes closed listen to the sounds around you. Listen beyond any manmade sounds to the sounds of nature.
- Whatever you saw before you closed your eyes, visualise the beauty of the area that often lies behind what we initially see.
- Absorb the positive energy from your location and open your eyes.

Whilst you are there are there any trees reflecting in the river? Or any boats going past? Think about what that might mean to you. Then turn to the study guide.

Chapter 19

MEDITATION
THE WOODS
Hidden Faces

Extension of **The Garden** meditation process but can be simplified as below in the woods.

- Find a comfortable safe place to sit and look around. What can you see and hear?
- Close your eyes. How has this changed what you feel and hear?
- After a few quiet minutes think about how your perception changed when you closed your eyes.
- Now open your eyes and look around you. Do you feel more in tune with your surroundings. Can you relate to anything that you can see?
- Look at the trees. They have faces!
- Each tree has a hidden face. I don't mean a man made one, but something natural to that tree.
- Why not give the tree a hug. They are very grounding especially if you have been floating away with your meditation!
- Trees each have their own aura and also a collective one. Maybe you haven't seen an aura yet. If not turn back to chapter 3 in the Study guide.

Take a few minutes to think about your experience and what that might mean to you.

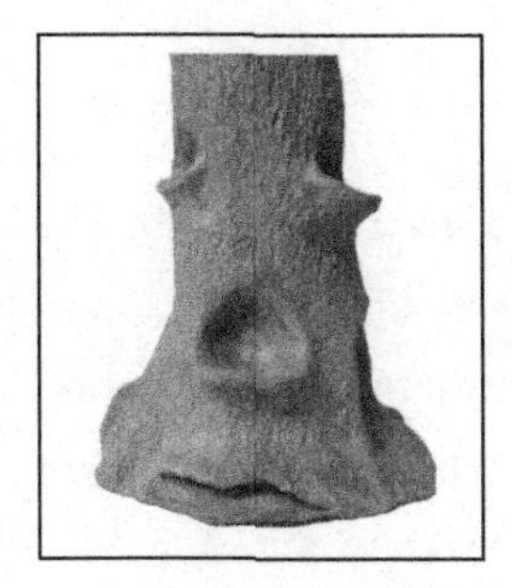

Chapter 20

WORKING THROUGH THE CHAKRAS

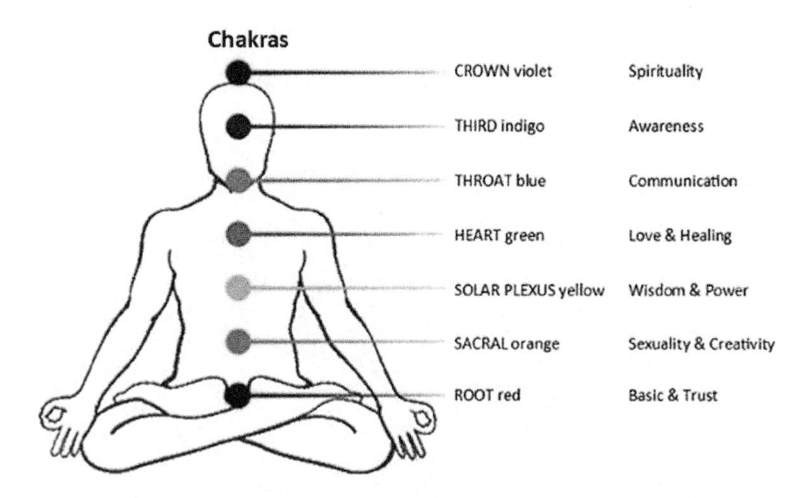

The Chakra colours correspond to the colours of the rainbow, with each having its own significance. The information here is basic – it's all you need to get going with working on those areas of your mind body and spirit. There is plenty of information online if you would like to delve into it further.

NOTE. Pink is not shown here, but it is the centre of the Green Heart Chakra.

RED	Root or Base. Grounds you to the Earth. Energy, passion, survival & stability.
ORANGE	Vitality, emotions, sexuality, happiness, desire, creativity & change.
YELLOW	Personal power. Will, wisdom, trusting our gut feelings, courage, confidence & abundance.
GREEN	Love, compassion, emotional balance, forgiveness, caring, healing, empathy
BLUE	Speaking the truth, verbal and non-verbal communication, self-expression.
INDIGO	Purple. Third Eye, Awareness, divine wisdom, psychic abilities, intuition, inspiration, imagination & trust higher self, perception.
VIOLET	White. Fusion of chakra energies. Connection to divine consciousness. Serenity. Knowing & Spirituality enlightenment.

Chapter 21

TRANSLATING IMAGES & SYMBOLS

By now you will have discovered many things: Boats, trees, paths, temples, water, **Guides**, gifts – the list is endless!

Chapter 21 in the Study Guide is dedicated to that.

You will also find more explanations in Part 3 The Journey.

GO TO THE STUDY GUIDE FOR THE GLOSSARY.

RECAP

Secret Garden Meditation
The short version!

*Before going into the **Garden** we have to release the negativity that surround us in our everyday life.*

Get comfortable and close your eyes.

Take a few deep breaths and still your mind.

Visualise a light coming in through your crown chakra (top of your head)

Fill your body with this light and then push it into your aura (through your chakra centres). Push the light out as far as possible, expanding and cleansing your aura. If there are any dark spaces visualise a starburst in these areas.

*When you are ready bring the light back inside and walk in front of you into the **Waterfall**.*

Let the water or tiny lights wash over you, cleansing the etheric body.

*When you are ready walk through the **Waterfall** into the **Cave** behind it. You will see a **Pool**. This is the **Pool** of healing. If you ever see anything in your **Garden** that you are uncomfortable with or that you want to get rid of, throw it into the **Pool** where it will transmute into positive energy.*

*Step towards the **Pool** and if you want to, jump in, and feel the water healing and comforting you.*

*When you are ready get out of the **Pool** and look around the **Cave** until you see a crack or opening in the rock. Walk through and find yourself in your **Garden**. Look about for your **Seat**. It may be a trunk, a wooden or iron **Seat**, a mound of grass or anything that you feel is right for you. When you find the **Seat** sit down and look around your **Garden**.*

What do you see, what can you hear?

What is the weather like, and what can you smell?

Take some time here and if you have a problem ask for help.

When you are ready walk back to the ***Cave****. Just outside the crack you will see something on the ground. This is your first gift from the* ***Garden****. Pick it up and bring it with you through the crack, into the* ***Cave****, through the* ***Waterfall*** *and back into your room.*

***

This is always the fore-runner of your entrance into the **Garden**. Each time you go into it see how it grows. Explore places you haven't been before, until you begin to know where everything is. It does not have to be a traditional **Garden**. There can be a beach, forest, or anything. It can be a **Garden** you know or something completely new. Go with it, do not try to manipulate it into something that you understand.

Now the rest is up to you!

For more clues of what else you might find, go to the Study Guide Glossary 'Translating Symbols'

or PART 3 THE JOURNEY

to read my story of what I found in my Garden at the beginning of my journey to find a better ME ☺

PART 2

SECRET GARDEN

THE STUDY GUIDE

SECRET GARDEN

THE STUDY GUIDE

HELLO!

I see you have turned to the Study Guide – hopefully to find out what each chapter means as you come to it.

As I mentioned at the start of the book I have done my best not to influence you – for you to create your own **Secret Garden** and not to just copy mine!! So it is important at first to follow the book as instructed.

Everything in your **Garden** has a purpose; you just have to know how to recognise the signs. So to that end I have created this section in my book to help you with that.

It is organised in corresponding chapters. So it's a good idea just to work through one chapter at a time in your workbook, then turn to this study guide to get the best from this book.

So let's start with a few **AFFIRMATIONS & SAYINGS**

Chapter 1

If it's uncomfortable shift position.

What do you think this means?

This came to me during a Meditation when I was trying to deal with something difficult. It could mean simply that you are meditating in an uncomfortable position. But on a deeper level it could mean that something in your life is uncomfortable even unresolvable – so look at it from a different position / perspective. Are you looking at the situation one sided or do you need to leave that situation completely? Do you need to shift your position on the situation?

Let it go, and if it was yours to start with it will come back to you.

Imagine that you have just let your doves free. You trust them to come home, but inevitably some don't make it back. That is like people. We sometimes hang onto relationships that have long since broken down. It's hard to let go, but by doing so, if they are meant to be in your life they will come back.

NOTES. Chapter 1

HOW WE SEE OURSELVES

The Spider and the Fly - Just which one do you think you are, are you the same in other's eyes?

1) What are your thoughts on this, how do you see yourself, the spider, or the fly? Did others see you the same way?

We can all become embroiled in other people's dramas or create some of our own. We may find it difficult to remove ourselves from the web they spin, and sometimes it seems impossible.

But to be aware of situations, and where we stand in it helps us to find a way to resolve them.

2) What do you see when you look in the mirror? Are you smiling?

You are the most important person in your life – without you, no one has you. Remember this when you look in the mirror.

Self-worth and well-being are very important to us as humans. Yet with busy lifestyles we often don't take the time to look after ourselves. So smile at yourself – you are worth it!

Chapter 1

EXERCISE 0. Calming Breath

1) How did you get on with this? Were you able to still your mind?

2) **Tip** Here is an idea which might help if you are struggling to focus.

When you start to meditate to calm your mind, think about something which is featureless or still – I visualise an iceberg which I photographed when I was in Alaska.

Chapter 1

EXERCISE 1. Colour Me

When you are ready draw or colour how you feel. You don't have to be Picasso or Dali. It can be a match stick person with colours around, or just the colours if that is what you feel. Try not to 'make' it happen. Just be spontaneous.

Take a look at your picture.

What was it of? Did you draw a person? Or just a page of colour?

What colours did you use? Or did you just use a black pencil?

There are some notes below but look at the chapter in this guide on Chakras for a more detailed description of colour.

TRANSLATING YOUR DRAWING

Were you in a box or enclosed in a shape? You are feeling **Trapped.** Think about why.

Did you seem to be floating or maybe have no legs? You are **Ungrounded** - go for a walk in the Park or your Garden, hug a tree or dig in your Garden.

Lots of colour but no actual person? **Ungrounded**

Several people and you are the smallest? **Self-worth.** Feeling insignificant or unimportant - or that those around you are more important than you. If you were the largest then perhaps you feel more important to those around you. You were all equal size? **Good balance**

Soft or Rounded shapes - **Happiness or love** good sign.

Pointed jagged or erratic lines - **Anger or frustration.** something needs dealing with before / or because it causes you stress.

Spirals and circles - **Caught in a loop.** Are you going round and round and don't seem to be getting anywhere? Shift Position.

Colours used with these shapes can confirm the meaning or show you a resolution.

For example

The man is trapped. He feels overwhelmed but he can see that growth is possible. He just needs to find a way to get there.
Black and white drawing implies reluctance to engage.
If the box was yellow or orange that could indicate emotions, red could be frustration or anger, blue could be communication.
The wave could be communication if it was blue, red could be strength, anger, or frustration. And love and harmony if the trees were green.
More information on colour in Chakras chapter 20

Once you have had a go at translating your picture, take some time to reflect on it.

Chapter 2

EXERCISE 2. Body Scan

PART 1

This is quite self-explanatory. It involves tensing or tightening your muscles and working your way up your body and visualising releasing your tension and negativity through the top of your head – your Crown Chakra. Where does that tension go – into the atmosphere, ether, or space as vibrantly as a jet, or gently as smoke, stars, or anything else that you sense as you are doing it.

PART 2

When you are totally relaxed you visualise a wall of golden light at your feet. It looks solid but as you watch it you will see it begin to move very slowly.

Imagine a photo copier, x ray or the scanner on your printer. It's as if when the scanner moves it takes an image of the energy surrounding your body. If it gets stuck in a specific place this is a block. These are usually in your aura but could be physically felt too and it could relate to a previous injury.

Were you able to do this Exercise?

Did you find any blocks – could you release them? Did you find out what caused them?

***

When you are doing the body scan it helps to lie down – so it's good to do when you go to bed as it helps you to relax for sleep.

The reason why you release the energy through your crown is so that it doesn't get stuck anywhere else in the body and it then disperses into the ether as positive energy.

Some people, especially those that have learned other techniques, might find it difficult to release the energy through their crown chakra, and have been taught to take it downwards through their feet into the earth. If this is easier then take the energy down and out through the soles of your feet.

NOTES FOR CHAPTERS 3 & 4

Gaining the Keys to the Kingdom
The Cleansing & The Waterfall

WHAT ARE........ Aura, Chakras, & Karma.

What is your knowledge regarding these terms? Did you know what they were before you did this course? A basic knowledge of these things is fine, but if you would like to find out more than is written in this book there are many websites for some online research.

More about **Chakras** will be coming in Chapter 20 of this Workbook and the Study Guide, and an article I wrote for a magazine will cover **Karma** and can be found in part 3 **The Journey**.

Aura

Auras look like a 'halo' that surrounds the body in different colours but often seen with the naked eye as a light coloured glow, or ripple. The colours that surround the body are the same as the Chakras (see chapter 20) starting with red closest to the body.

But can we see or feel them? Kirlian photography is said to show the colours in our aura but there is much speculation over that, however I think we can feel it. Think about when you are playing a game, and someone creeps up behind you – you instantly know that they are there, and you turn to find them. Try this with a friend and see how long it takes before you know they are there. How close are they before they enter your aura, and you feel them?

As you practise your Cleansing Exercise 3 does that distance change? Is it different with a close friend or someone you don't know well?

One physical technique for cleansing the aura is to Smudge.

This is done with a bundle of herbs, often sage, tightly bound and then lit to create smoke. That is then blown or wafted with a feather or similar around your body into your aura. It is often associated with the indigenous peoples of America and Canada.

It is a lovely thing to have done. The smell and sense of peace is wonderful. Much has been written on Auras so more information can be gained by a quick search on the internet.

But.....why not learn how to see them yourself?

HOW TO SEE AURAS

Have you ever looked at a magic eye picture? They sometimes help us to be able to see auras. If you would like to try go to https://www.magiceye.com/How_to_see_printer_version.htm it gives you the instructions of how to do it, with an example.

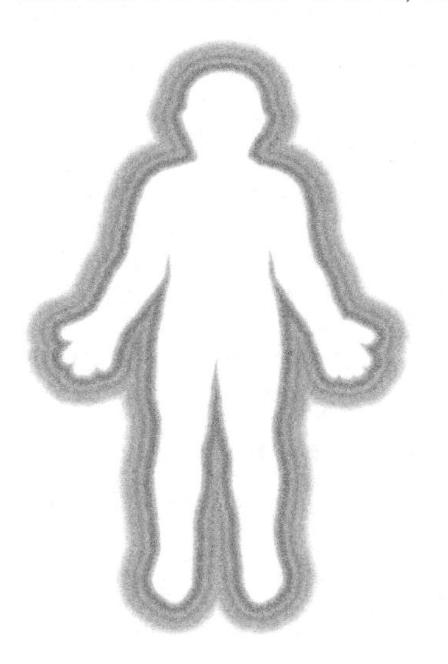

Finding auras can be done in much the same way. You look beyond the person or object that you are trying to find the aura of.

Don't forget: If you want to look at a person's aura ask them first for permission. Then ask them to stand by a blank wall. Lighter is best then you may more easily see the colours. Don't expect to see them at first, some people need some practice, and colours may take a bit longer. You have to focus your mind. You may first see the light 'shadow' or ripple. Tree auras are the easiest to see because when you look up at them they are against a blank background of sky.

I could see auras clearly until I had a cataract operation about 20 years ago. The wonderful surgeon who played loud classical music before he did his ops asked me how I was getting on when I went for my check-up. I said that I could see for miles – further than I ever could in my life, everything had sharp edges again, it was wonderful but...I could no longer see auras. He was fascinated. Over the years I have trained my eyes to see them again but unfortunately not now in colour.

WHY DO I FEEL..... A pressure in my head when I am meditating. This can happen sometimes if you are focusing a bit too hard. So you could try relaxing the Brow Chakra. **This is how:**

Brow Chakra Exercise: Raise your forehead. Relax your forehead as you scrunch up your eyes and cheeks. Hold for a few seconds and release. Then stretch your face by opening your mouth wide and stretching your chin down and raising your forehead. Take a deep breath and relax your face, head, neck, and shoulders as you let the breath out.

WHAT ARE..... Keys to the Kingdom? These are gained through self-reflection and visualisation. They open parts of your **Secret Garden**.

WHAT IS..........That Feeling that something is missing?

This could be a type of homesick feeling, or that you have missed something, or something is no longer there. It's as if part of you is missing and often no matter what we have in our lives that feeling is still there.

As you become more in tune with who you are, that feeling usually fades.

When I worked with young children many would tell me they felt like this when they got to the age of 8 or 9 years old, some said they felt like they were going to die. I believe this to be the releasing of the tight bond a child has with its parent as it becomes part of a new social order of school, teachers, and other children with different values to that which they have learnt at home. They are now getting ready for their journey into adulthood.

WHY THIS METHOD?

Many meditation and visualisation techniques exist but there is a specific process used for **SECRET GARDEN** work. Cold showers in the morning or evening releases the spirit from negativity. If you are at all concerned with the effect of this practice please consult your medical advisor beforehand. But I have known it to be a contributory factor in the healing of M.E. in several cases. The daily routine for entering your **Garden** is in the next section THE CLEANSING.

Chapter 3

EXERCISE 3. THE CLEANSING

You may already know how to meditate, but it makes no difference if you have never done it before, in fact, if you have you may find it difficult at first to do this process, as you will already have your own way of meditating.

It's like learning anything from bricklaying to crochet – in the end, we do it the way we feel most comfortable and build on the skills we have learnt. That's what we are doing now – building the skills.

The Cleansing meditation **Ex 3** becomes the final method here in chapter 3. It combines what you learnt in Exercise 0 with additional steps to give you what you need to get into your **Secret Garden**.

You may know when you are ready to bring the light down around you as it will be just above your head or hovering above you to one side. When you are ready surround yourself with that golden light in an egg-shaped (ovoid) space which is your aura.

If you feel your mind 'slipping' back into everyday issues like, what's for dinner or remembering to pay a bill, just be aware of your breathing again to refocus your mind.

As mentioned in the * ***AUTHORS NOTE*** *in the workbook there is an alternative to the cold shower.*

I am writing this book 30 years after my first venture into my **Secret Garden** and by now, having taught it to so many people I know the cold shower is not always a practical step for some people, either through health, time, or preference – so you can use the **Waterfall Ex 4** with **Ex 3** instead.

Chapter 4

EXERCISE 4. THE WATERFALL

Stand under it allowing the water of silver rain or tiny lights to wash over you to cleanse your etheric body, which directly surrounds your physical body – is like a flexible diving suit!

This exercise with Ex 3 makes up your meditation to get into the next stage of your journey.

How to make an Exit!

If you want to exit your meditation before moving on to the next Exercise, find your way back to the Waterfall, and as you leave it bring the light back inside, take some deep breaths, hold for a few moments then open your eyes and you will be back in your room.

It's best to finish a meditation with this otherwise you may feel disorientated.

Previous experience with Meditation

If you have ever followed a visualisation technique or meditation either face to face in a group, one-to-one, by audio, online or in a book you may find this quite different. It is. It is all about giving you the control and power to develop your own space. More about this coming up.

How do I get into my Secret Garden?

There are various things to learn first. See the next chapter, the **Cave** in your workbook.

Right on WE GO!

NOTES FOR CHAPTERS 5 & 6

Safe Sacred Space

The Cave & The Pool

The entrance to your **Garden** *is in the* **Cave** *and the safe space is in the* **Pool**. ....

Well done for making it this far - even if you went no further you have the tools for a more relaxing life.....

But why leave it here? The following exercises may well change your life!

So let's have a look at the **Protection Visualisations.**

As it says in the chapter, you may find yourself feeling light-headed after some meditations which take you a bit deeper. Imagine you are on a bus full of people with colds (I am sure you'll remember COVID!) You don't want to catch it so what do you do? You might wear a mask, sit on your own or catch the next bus.

In a similar way, we don't want to come out of meditation and enter a busy public area - we are a bit like the light that draws moths to its flame. We need to close down.

So the chapter gives 3 techniques.

I will give you one more way. When you exit the **Cave** and enter the **Waterfall** you can close down before you leave the safety of the water. Imagine you are an open rose or similar and visualise you are closing your petals.

There are other ways too, which we may get to during the course of this book. But for now, those 4 techniques will suffice. For younger adults who were keen Harry Potter readers, you might find the Invisibility cloak the best way! They all work but like everything in this book, you will find the right way for you.

Chapter 5

EXERCISE 5. THE CAVE

So are you getting used to the process? Only 1 more step to go after the **Cave** and you will see your **Secret Garden** for the first time.

As mentioned before, I could tell you what's in my **Cave** but then that would probably influence you and whilst searching for what I have shared of mine, you may miss what's in your own.

Did you have a good look about your **Cave**? Could you answer those questions in the workbook?

OK let's look at the inside of the **Cave**. What did you see? Could you see anything, or was it too dark? If there was light where was it coming from? What are the floor, walls and roof made of?

Were there any areas you could not access? Or places off of the main **Cave**?

Did you go anywhere else? Were there any colours? How did you feel?

Or were you not able to get into the **Cave** at all?

So let's look at some of these questions.

If you could not get into the **Cave**, then perhaps you still have work to do in the other chapters first. You might not be quite ready. Don't give up, keep working through the exercises until you manage to get through the **Waterfall** into the **Cave**. It could also be that you have some tough work to do in the **Cave** which is your inner self. This is the first and probably most powerful place to find 'Baggage' which you may not have wanted to deal with which could have been locked away. So this could be quite a big area for you to have to work on and being in the **Cave** might go on for some time.

Imagine an attic with lots of boxes that need sorting!

Don't worry, everyone gets to where they need to be at their own pace.

Sometimes we find our way into our **Secret Garden** then next time we can't get in because other things that we need to deal with have risen to the surface. Or we might fall asleep and again it's because we are not ready for that yet.

It can be a little frustrating when we have found our way into our **Garden** and have been working well finding and dealing with issues, then suddenly we are stuck in the **Cave** again! Just another box to sort out!

So What Are These Gifts?

You may often find a gift at the entrance to your ***Cave****. Usually when you leave but sometimes there might be something there as you enter, this will be of use to you in your meditation, either in the* ***Cave*** *or the* ***Garden*** *or for when you exit.*

The **Gifts** are **Guides** that we recognise as physical objects and something that you might need. Here are some examples.

Coins – Abundance. Do you have a financial issue to resolve? Or will they help you to make a decision? Or put it in your pocket as a lucky coin.

Flowers – It all depends on what they are and their colour. Could be growth, which usually reminds you that there is beauty in everything. Was it a rose with thorns? Maybe a warning about a prickly situation.

Crystals – Colours and types have different meanings. There is a Crystal meditation in the workbook.

Boats – These are opportunities and are usually found on the River (we will get to that later.)

Words – These are the easiest to understand because they often tell us directly what they mean. However, sometimes they take a bit of working out!

See **Glossary Chapter 21** in the Study Guide for more examples.

So what happens when we find something we don't like....well, I will get to that in the next Chapter – The **Pool**.

Chapter 6

EXERCISE 6. THE POOL

*The **Pool** is your safe place. If there is ever anything in your **Secret Garden** or **Cave** that you do not want there then it can be thrown into the **Pool** where it will transmute to positive energy and be released from your **Cave**. It won't return to your **Garden** or your **Pool**.*

Am I safe? You are in control in your **Garden**. There are safety nets – the main one is your **Pool**.

What was your experience?

Did you find the **Pool**? What's your **Pool** like? What could you hear? Did you get into it? Was it relaxing?

Was it a full-size swimming **Pool**, or more of a puddle? It can be anything, but it usually evolves to suit your **Cave**. It could change now and then, getting larger or changing shape to incorporate other areas but after some time it will settle into something you know and are happy with and can use any time you wish as this is the place for your healing process.

Did you throw anything into the **Pool**? What happened? Did you see it turn into positive energy? Where did it go? Again I don't want to tell you too much so as not to influence you. But later you can learn more from Part 3 The Journey.

Suffice to say, you need an exit for the energy so that you can visualise it leaving your **Cave** - unless you decide to turn it into something useful in your **Cave** or **Secret Garden**. Think about when we release negative energy from our body through our crown Chakra. The negative energy which is released from your **Pool** could leave your **Cave** from its own crown chakra – perhaps an exit at the top of the **Cave?** Maybe it's better to send it into the universe rather than storing it in the Earth. We don't want to increase the problems we already have here! But if you manage to convert it into something positive, this won't be a problem.

What about People?

Well, you can throw them in the **Pool** too! Don't worry it won't do them any physical harm but can change your relationship on a higher level which in turn can change your physical relationship. I will get to that later too in the Ego chapter. People don't usually enter your **Secret Garden** if you haven't visualised them there - except for your **Guides.** If you are having some issues with a person you can invite them into your **Cave** and put them into the **Pool**. Any bad energy will transmute to positive energy like with the objects you have thrown in. Usually, they go then, or you can ask them to leave if you want to.

How can I change the past?

We can't change our past or what others have done to us, but we can change the way we deal with or think about it. We can do this in the **Cave**.

NOTE

Something I have found over the years is that if a person is not ready for a meditation they are learning, they will fall asleep. If this happens to you, don't worry, just continue to work on the previous meditations and Ex 3-5 a bit longer then try again.

Next, it's time to finally find out how you get into your Secret Garden!

NOTES FOR CHAPTERS 7 & 8

Safe Sacred Space
The Seat & The Garden

And Finally the ***Secret Garden***

To be relaxed is essential not only for Meditation, but for Life itself. Meditation helps to align our mind, body, and spirit, which in turn enhances our lives, making us happier, healthier, and more fulfilled.

At the same time, it makes us more aware of our surroundings, other people, and the planet we live on. We are tenants here on Earth, doing the best we can. But we could do more, and by being in tune with our mind body and spirit we can work on multi-dimensions, instead of just in the physical.

Remember if there is ever anything in your **Garden** that you don't want there just take it back to the **Cave** and throw it into the **Pool** where it will transmute to positive energy.

We are now at the beginning of an incredible journey, one that you can come back to time and time again. I have been on this journey for over 30 years, and I still clearly remember what I discovered in those early. Those first lessons of who I am, those first resolutions with past events and my first look at my **Garden**.

This is your time now. But first, you have to find somewhere to sit!

Chapter 7

EXERCISE 7. THE SEAT

This is where it all begins. The **Seat** *is really the first stop in the* **Garden**. *It is a very important* **Seat**. *You can resolve any problem here. It is a meeting place too where you can get help from your* **Guides**. *It is essential that this is found before going on as without our* **Seat** *we often do not find where we are going.*

How are you doing with your Cleansing routine?

Do you still feel a bit disorientated or not quite focused? If so pop into the **Pool** before leaving your **Cave**, that will resolve any issues there.

Did you find your **Seat**? What does it look like? Where is it?

This is a place that you will become very familiar with over time.

Was anyone there waiting for you? If so that was a Guide. They will help you in your **Garden**, but more about them later.

It is important from now on to use your notepad to jot things down after each meditation. Something might come to you that you don't understand right away but as you move through the Exercises your notes should make more sense. For example, a book reference. Sometimes you will be shown a book which you recognise from your physical bookshelf or given a reference to look up. It might say 3rd blue book from left, page 23 line 4*. Look it up. It could be a very relevant sentence, or it might not make any sense right now but could guide you later on.

*Authors Note – *I chose that book reference at random whilst writing this page – so I checked it out a few days later.... The words were 'I promise.' Well, I did! I promised 30 years ago to write this book. See how it works?*

Chapter 8

EXERCISE 8. THE GARDEN

We have finally arrived at our destination. But this is just the beginning!
In your ***Secret Garden*** *are many things and each time you go in you will see it grow.*
It does not have to be a traditional ***Garden****.*

You are here at last! Did you get into your **Garden**? If not don't worry, there is still more for you to do in the **Cave** or on your **Seat** before you get in. Try again soon after doing a bit more work with previous meditations.

If you got in what was your first impression of your **Garden**? Do you recognise it? Or is it somewhere you have never been before?

Doesn't matter! It's your **Secret Garden** and will evolve into something fantastic. This early view might stay the same or change completely. Don't try to make that happen just go with it. The more you explore the more you will find.

It's time to be observant. What else did you find? What objects did you see?

Did you meet anyone there? Did they show you around? Or did you explore on your own?

What was the weather like? What was the time of year? What was the main colour?

Were there any fences or boundaries? Did they stop you from exploring? As time goes on you will be able to remove them in various ways – or if that seems too difficult climb over or walk round! They are just your barriers. You are in control!

Did you get any messages?

What does it feel like to be in your **Secret Garden** at last?

EXERCISE 8b. COLOUR MY SECRET GARDEN

So time to draw your **Garden**, as you did in your Self pictures in Chapter 1.

Some people draw a pictorial image, others draw a floorplan and others draw a combination of both.

I am so tempted to add mine here but again, I don't want to influence you.

It is your **Garden,** not mine 

Although I painted the cover image, it is not my **Secret Garden**, but it is a place that I visited.

Your **Garden** is yours in any form that you create. It is Secret for that reason, something that no one else can see.

NOTES FOR CHAPTER 9

The Guides

Who and What are they?

*Our **Guides** are people or creatures in our **Garden** that help us to learn about ourselves, and to help resolve our issues. This is the last piece of the basic **Secret Garden** technique. You now have all the tools you need to embark on your Journey of Discovery to find YOU.*

There are people in our lives that influence or help us, but they are not always positive. But in our **Garden,** our **Guides** may take human, animal, or inanimate form, such as books or gifts we find and are always there to help us – even though a little challenging sometimes!

Feel free to question what comes from them.

Chapter 9

EXERCISE 9. THE GUIDES

Who have you found so far? Start to make a glossary by listing anything you remember about each one. Name, form they take, where you see them, and any messages they give you.

Also, make a list of the gifts/objects that you find and where you found them e.g. **Cave**, **Garden**, by **Seat** etc. and what you think they mean.

Did you ask for help with anything? Did you get help? Write it down.

It is easy to forget those small things at the beginning. By writing it down you can look back and work on particular things as you go along.

What did you do with your **Guides**? Did you sit with them, or walk with them, or did they show you something important?

How do you feel in your **Garden** with your **Guides**?

You have done the basics for Secret Garden. Now your adventure REALLY begins!

SECTION 2 THE MEDITATIONS

SEEING OUR GARDEN GROW

The following Meditations are interactive and can be used in any order.

Now that you have all 6 basic elements (shown in bold throughout): **Waterfall, Cave, Pool, Seat, Garden, and Guides**, you can use the rest of the meditations in any order you wish, depending on either what you need or what you are drawn to – that really amounts to the same thing!

As it says in the workbook if you are not ready for that particular Meditation you may fall asleep. However, if on the other hand you keep getting interrupted, it could be that you are either not ready for it, or that you have had obstacles in your life stopping you from dealing with that real situation. Only you know the answer. If you don't, go and sit on your **Seat** and ask why it is so difficult to deal with it.

In the following chapters, there will be lots of questions to jog your memory. It's important now to be observant. Remember to write it down. There are clues to the Meditations but not much in the Study Guide chapters as I don't want to influence you. You will find some answers in the **Translating Symbols Glossary** at the end of this Study Guide, and you will find more answers in **THE JOURNEY**, part 3 of this book.

Enjoy the Meditations, do those which you are drawn to or feel that they will help in some way. Come back and do more at other times. This is a lifelong technique which you can tap into at any time.

NOTES FOR CHAPTER 10

EXERCISE 10. MEDITATION
The Crystal
Transformation – Facets of the Self

The Crystal represents you.
All the facets of your personality, your thoughts, your mind, your Ego, your body – your Self.
Do you know that ***YOU*** *are the most important person? Without you no one else has you.*

We are in the **Cave** by the **Pool** to do this meditation.

Did you know that you are the most important person? Sometimes this meditation can bring up emotional feelings when we understand self-worth. It isn't 'selfish' to care about yourself because then you can care for others without it being harmful to your own health. How does that feel?

The Crystal Meditation is a great tool for finding out who we are. Imagine a crystal with many facets. That's who we are, a many-faceted being. We are different to different people. We have a side that we show to close friends, another to family, another to those we don't know, another to work colleagues.

I have had friends who thought they knew me but didn't know me at all. Some people see what they want to see. But do we do that too? Do we believe how important we are to ourselves and others?

So the Crystal is a way to be clearer about who we are.

Don't try to clean the whole crystal at the same time – it is huge! Look at it and clean the facet which you are drawn to. There are many ways to clean it. Water from your **Pool**, sand, stones, or a piece of fabric. Give it a good rub, it won't scratch – it's as tough as diamond. Maybe it is Diamond!

How does it feel now that the facet is clean? You have spent time lovingly caring for it. Do you do that in your day-to-day life?

It's time to do that.

NOTES FOR CHAPTER 11

EXERCISE 11. MEDITATION
The Hot Air Balloon
Freedom

We often allow people and situations to hold us back in our lives. We can free ourselves from that by cutting the ropes that bind us. Once we are free from those constricting ties, those that are meant to be in our lives will come back.

Did you find your Hot Air Balloon in your **Garden**? What colour was it?

How big was it?

Could you get into the basket?

Did you manage to cut those ties?

What were they like, thin strings or metal cables as you find on a suspension bridge?

Were there many? How long did it take to cut them?

What did you use to cut them with? Was that in the basket somewhere?

Did your hot air balloon leave the earth and float upwards? How did it feel to be free?

What was the weather like?

Were you in the basket alone?

What could you see?

What happened next?

NOTES FOR CHAPTER 12

EXERCISE 12. MEDITATION
Temple of Knowledge
Living Library & Akashic Records

This is the Living Library. The ever-changing books of our lives. It's the place to find out why we are here. Where we can look back and perhaps forward. It holds all the books of all the people that have lived. Your book is there. This is the only book that you will be able to read.

So what are the Akashic Records: Think of them as interactive Books of Life in the form of a library that stores all the information of every individual human and other life forms that have ever lived on Earth since the creation of our planet. Like a super-computer, it holds all of the words, emotions, thoughts, and events that have ever happened in the past, present, or future. To access our own Book of Life in the Akashic records can give us an insight into what influences us in our everyday life and can show how we are connected to others around us.

Did you find the Temple in your **Garden**? Were there obstacles?

Don't worry if you did not find it at first. Keep checking as it will appear when you are ready.

Where was it? What did it look like? How many floors did have? Could you see the roof?

You might like to draw it and add that to your other drawings.

How difficult was it to get to it?

Could you get in? Did it have a door? What was the door like?

What was the interior like? Were there windows?

Did you find somewhere to sit in the sun?

Did you find your book? How did you find it? How did you know it was yours?

What colour was it? Was it thick or thin? What was the cover like?

What were the pages made from? What colour were they?

Did you see any writing in it? What was the writing like? Were there blank pages?

What did your book say?

Did you put the book back or leave it somewhere?

Did you try to take it with you? What stopped you?

Did you try to read someone else's book? What happened?

Was it easy to leave the Library?

Did you go and sit on your **Seat** or go straight back through the **Waterfall**?

Have you tried to go back to the library since your first visit?

What happened?

NOTES FOR CHAPTER 13

EXERCISE 13. MEDITATION
The Giving Tree
Abundance

Abundance is to have more than you need and comes in many forms. It is not always about financial gain. It can be the love of friends and family, the feeling of goodwill when you have been able to help someone, or they have helped you, it can be receiving a gift or being able to share with others.

This tree can take many forms and be anywhere in your **Garden**.

It might not be noticeable at first but if you ask for something you will be drawn towards it.

There are many ways to access the abundance too.

You may feel like climbing the tree or sitting under it or just watching it from your **Seat**. Each person's adventure here is different.

Did you find your Tree? Where was it? Where were you?

What did it look like? Were there leaves or bare branches?

Did you ask for something? Did you see anything hanging in the tree? Or on the ground under the tree?

Was your abundance obvious or symbolic? Or was it a thought to help you?

Could you bring it with you when you left your **Garden**?

The Glossary in Chapter 21 of the Study Guide could hold some answers.

NOTES FOR CHAPTER 14

MEDITATION
Heart Light
Healing Love

Sometimes we have to deal with emotional ties with family, friends, or other people. Sometimes there are issues to be worked out and other times we might just want to show our love to those close to us. We cannot change what has happened in the past, but we can change the energy around situations and within ourselves.

So we are now back in the **Cave** by the **Pool** again to do some work, this time on relationships with others.

Healing Relationships

How many people did you want to work with? Did you want to work with more than 3? How many came? Did you work on them individually?

Were you able to feel the light coming from your heart towards the person in front of you?

What happened when you sent to heart light to them?

Were you able to close the heart light after sending it to each person?

How did you do that? Did you use a veil?

What happened after each healing? Where did the person go?

Did you take anyone into the **Pool**? Did you go in as well?

Did they leave easily? What did you do after they left?

Cont

Healing Situations

Was this meditation more about a situation that has occurred in the past? If so, did you work on one at a time until it was resolved?

It is similar to the heart light but this time you sent that healing love light into that event or situation and perhaps the people involved.

Was the situation clear? How did you see it? As a movie, thought process, a conversation or something else?

Did it involve people? Were you able to talk to them or the event about what happened?

Did you have any control over the outcome? If so what could you have done differently? If not how can you change how you feel about it?

What could have happened in your life without that event? What can you envisage could happen in the future if you could let it go? What will happen if you don't?

Think of the options and how you can move forward in a more positive way. We may not be able to control what happened in our lives, but we can control how we think about them, which in turn can change future events.

Authors Note

When I was younger I was in a very negative and violent relationship. It caused me to lose my confidence and be afraid, but if not for that relationship I would not have relocated, and my daughter may not be here. As I sit writing this, looking out over the beautiful green in front of my house from my office window I know that I would not have changed the events in my life. Because if they had not happened I may not be living in such a lovely place and my daughter might not have been born. She and I have had the most amazing adventures and she is my best friend. So the way I changed my past was to reflect on the positive things that evolved from that short relationship 40 years ago.

NOTES FOR CHAPTER 15

EXERCISE 15. MEDITATION
The Inner Sanctuary
Deep Inside The Cave – TRUE YOU.

Somewhere in your ***Cave,*** *there is a hidden room or space. Here you can work on the deepest level on things hidden away even from your Self. Work here is not always easy and if you find it too difficult leave and come back another time when you are ready.*

Well, you are back in the **Cave** for this one. Have a good look around. This may not be an easy place to find, and you might think you have found it, but it might just be another area in your **Cave**, or it could be accessed from your **Cave** and found somewhere in your **Garden**. It could take you months or even years to find it, and you might only go there once, because what you find will be so powerful that you will always remember it. It really is one of the biggest lessons. And what you change here will affect your life.

You might find your Inner Child, a relationship, or part of you that you instinctively know is there / missing / or overwhelming and it's always out of reach. It's here you will find it! Come back again if you don't get in this time. You might suddenly be there one day when you are meditating and least expect it.

So have you found it? How long did it take – was it a space or a room? What did it look like? Was it comfortable?

What do you look like? Were there any objects in the space? Did you change anything in yourself or your space?

Could you leave easily?

What happened?

NOTES FOR CHAPTER 16

MEDITATION
The Sacred Mountain
Wisdom beyond limits

To get to our mountain we have to break down walls and fences, it's a long way and we may have to think beyond our limits, but we CAN make it.

We start in the **Garden** on the **Seat** looking for the Mountains distance.

Did you see them? What happened next?

Did you make your way there alone? Or with one of your **Guides**? Or did it seem too far away? Did you know that you can visualise yourself closer, or even there? Although the Journey might be the most important part of this experience.

Did you take anything with you, or find what you needed on the way?

Were there obstacles in your way? Did you have to overcome walls and fences? How did you do that?

Did you get to the top of the mountain or just part way up?

Did you meet anyone when you got there? What happened?

Do you understand what the lesson or message was about?

As mentioned in the workbook, this part of your Journey is unique to you, and you can go back up the mountain as many times as you wish to continue with whatever this lesson is.

Don't forget to write it down.

You will read about my mountain experience in Part 3 The Journey.

NOTES FOR CHAPTERS 17

MEDITATION
The Path & The White House
Family - Our Roots

In our **Garden** *just out of sight, perhaps along a path that we have not yet seen, is a White House where we find family and the lessons we have been given by them.*
It's time to finally face those lessons.

I didn't find my White House for some years, and when I did it was a wonderful experience. Had I found it earlier, it probably wouldn't have been. We find the right things at the right time in our **Garden**.

Did you find your White House and Path? Did the Path lead to the House?

Where were they? Describe their location. Is it always there now?

Could you find it again if you tried to go back?

Did it look like a Home that you remember? Or one that you would have liked it to be? Did you enter the House?

Who was at the House?

What happened? What did you need to do? Was it easy or difficult?

Did you leave quickly or enjoy your time there?

What happened next?

NOTES FOR CHAPTERS 18 & 19

EXTENDING THE BOUNDARIES

Location meditations

There are two last meditations that .. take you outside your meditation space into the real world: The River & The Woods. These meditations can be very powerful and are often enjoyed with other people.

It is good sometimes to enjoy meditating outside in specific locations: by the River, in the Woods, at the Beach and in your own back **Garden**. Always remember though when meditating outside your usual space, make sure that you are in a safe environment, with someone else or somewhere where you will not be disturbed.

NOTES FOR CHAPTER 18

MEDITATION
The River
Reflections

So did you find a nice quiet area at the River? How did you feel?

What was it like? Was it clean and tidy or covered in litter and rubbish? How did the state of the river make you feel?

What could you hear? Were the sounds natural like the wind or birds singling or were the sounds manmade?

If it was littered and noisy were you able to block that out when you had your eyes closed and listening to nature sounds?

Were you able to visualise and absorb the beauty of the area?

One of the Trees on the river bank is you. Did you see any trees reflected in the river?

Did you notice how big they were compared to the tree on the bank?

If the reflection was bigger than the tree itself, think about the people in your life. Have you given your power away to them, or let them overpower you in some way? They are the reflection.

Now focus on something important to you e.g. a project or something that you have been trying to do. What happened whilst you were focusing on the projects?

Did a boat go past and sent ripples out across your thoughts? Are you being distracted when trying to focus? Is that what is happening each time you try to work on your project?

There will often be many things that try to distract you or stop you from achieving your goals. Decide which is the most important - your project or something else. Then focus on that.

NOTES FOR CHAPTER 19

MEDITATION
The Woods
Hidden Faces

This was always my favourite location workshop when I was running my **Secret Garden** Groups. I live quite close to a Forest and closer to a park with lots of trees. I would take my group there to find some peace and quiet and look for an interesting tree.

If you refer back to the Notes in Chapter 3 in this study guide you will find the Seeing Auras section useful here.

Have a go when you next look at a tree – see if you can see its aura.

Finding the hidden Tree Faces is, for many people, easier than looking for the Tree aura.

So go to the Woods or the Park and walk about for a while until you find a comfortable **Seat** or place to stand next to the trees around you.

Close your eyes and listen. Can you hear the trees? They might be rustling or whooshing in the wind.

How does that make you feel?

Now open your eyes and look about.

Can you see a tree with what looks like a face? If not move a few feet away till you find one. They all seem to have them somewhere higher or lower amongst the branches, they just need finding.

Can you see its eyes, nose, mouth, and maybe even arms?

Did you touch or hug the tree? What did it feel like?

Do you feel more grounded?

NOTES FOR CHAPTER 20

WORKING THROUGH THE CHAKRAS

The Chakra colours correspond to the colours of the rainbow, with each having its own significance.

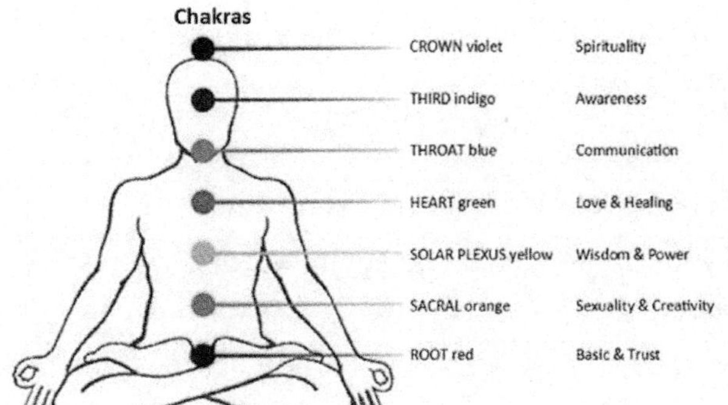

RED	Root or Base. Grounds you to the Earth. Energy, passion, survival & stability.
ORANGE	Vitality, emotions, sexuality, happiness, desire, creativity & change.
YELLOW	Personal power. Will, wisdom, trusting our gut feelings, courage, confidence & abundance.
GREEN	Love, compassion, emotional balance, forgiveness, caring, healing, empathy
BLUE	Speaking the truth, verbal and non-verbal communication, self-expression.
INDIGO	Purple. Third Eye, Awareness, divine wisdom, psychic abilities, intuition, inspiration, imagination & trust higher self, perception.
VIOLET	White. Fusion of chakra energies. Connection to divine consciousness. Serenity. Knowing & Spirituality enlightenment.

NOTE. Pink is not shown here, but it is the centre of the Green Heart Chakra.
A larger illustration is in Chapter 20 of the Workbook

It is a good idea when you finish meditating to close down your Chakras.

There are many ways to do this but here are 2 of my preferred ways.

1) Visualise each Chakra centre from root or base chakra to crown or head chakra and one by one encircle them with Golden Light and close them as you would close your eye. Leave a thin strand of light coming from your crown chakra to keep you connected to your higher self.

2) Imagine that your chakras are flowers, a lotus or water lily works well. They have been fully open whilst meditating and one by one from the root to the crown close them until they are each a bud.

Chapter 21

GLOSSARY: TRANSLATING IMAGES & SYMBOLS

You will also find more examples in Part 3 The Journey and Reflections at the end.

In a workshop situation, we would be able to discuss what objects or images we received in our meditation. We obviously cannot do that individually here and by now you will have discovered many things, so to help you to understand I have made a list of the most common symbols and the 6 elements. They may relate to more than one Exercise.

Garden	This is your private place to work on your life and what you want in it.
Seat	The place where you can view your **Garden**. It can be anything: rock, wall, grass, tree trunk - whatever you choose.
Waterfall	Where we cleanse our etheric body so that we can think and act more clearly and start the healing process
Cave	Sacred Space where we deal with emotions, memories and sometimes deeper issues.
Pool	of healing is in the **Cave**, where it transmutes unwanted thoughts, ideas, objects, and people into positive energy.
Guides	Helpers with you in the **Garden**: beings may not be human; they may even be animals. Ask them questions as this is the only way you learn!
Gifts	These are important objects which you find or are given. They have meanings depending on what they are. See below
Bat	represents Shamanic death, the end of the old life and your identity in that life. It is also a symbol of rebirth. It is time to let go of all that is outdated and done and to face your fears and move forward.
Boats	These are opportunities and are usually found on the River

Coins	Abundance. Do you have a financial issue to resolve? Or will they help you to make a decision? Or put it in your pocket for later.
Crystals	Colours and types have different meanings. But often they relate to facets of our being. There is a Crystal Meditation Chapter 10 in the workbook.
Flowers	It all depends on what they are and their colour. Could be growth, which usually reminds you that there is beauty in everything. Was it a rose with thorns? Maybe you are about to get stung by something financial. Or warning you about a prickly situation.
Inner sanctuary	A place to look or meditate deeply into who you are.
Lightworking	The role of a lightworker is to help each soul to grow and guide mankind along their life path to receive light and healing and a better understanding of our planet. This will raise the human race to a new multi-dimensional consciousness, which will heal us and our planet.
Message	All messages are there to help. They may come in many ways: in your meditation, or written on a paper you find, or given by a guide.
Paths	Your direction
Temple of Knowledge.	A large building full of books of life, including your book. Open it up and read what it says inside.
Temples	Significant places for learning
The Etheric body	is one of the main energy bodies that form the human energy system and is said to extend about 5cm from the physical body, to which it gives vitality.
Trees	Trees are about growth or seeing clearly – 'can't see the wood for the trees.'
Water	Any water e.g. river, pond, sea. Is it Flowing or stagnant, gently lapping, or are there stormy waves? Is this part of your journey difficult or easy?
Words	These are the easiest to understand because they often tell us directly what they mean. However, sometimes they take a bit of working out!

The Journey Continues

Think about how you will use your **Secret Garden**. How will it help you in your life and your work?

What was your biggest lesson and what did you like best?

Are there things which you would have liked more information on, or that you would have liked included in this book?

For Example, your work through **Secret Garden** may have brought up other thoughts and issues including:

Channelling, automatic writing, Past Lives & Reincarnation, Other Worlds & Beings including Extra Terrestrials, clairaudience, clairvoyance, Astral travel, Out of Body experiences, or how to stop that annoying dog next door from barking!

Well, I had to finish writing it at some point – it already took me nearly half my life to finally publish it! So you could research these questions on the internet – you will find everything there or join my **Secret Garden** Facebook Group and ask your questions. I will answer if I can. Contact details are at the back of the book.

I have been with my **Secret Garden** for over 30 years and although I think I could map it completely, there may still be areas that I don't know, that will come to me when the time is right. I have had many great adventures, and helped many people to find their own way and I am glad that this book is finally written to help others that I couldn't possibly have met otherwise.

So as you see it is a continuing process.

What we are trying to do is to 'grow' our **Secret Garden**, which is the way we want our life to be on a holistic level.

Within drawings and Visualisation and perhaps later building the **Garden** as a craft project we are actively trying to change our world.

We may see it as having walls and boundaries, the obstacles that hold us back, or we may find something there, which may be events or people from our past, that we still have to deal with.

We may find a beautiful balanced **Garden** with radiant sunshine and colourful flowers and there may appear to be very little to do until we open a door or find something hidden in the grass which leads us to yet another adventure on our Journey.

You may start to notice strange coincidences or synchronistic events in your everyday life, leading to opportunities which would have gone unnoticed without your **Garden**.

Secret Garden is a whole experience!

There are still lots of things for you to do.

* Work on your **Secret Garden** regularly.
* Now and then draw new Self and **Garden** pictures. It's good to look back to where it all started.
* Make a miniature model version of your **Secret Garden.**
* Who were you when you started to work with **Secret Garden**? What or who led you to be that person. Who are you now?
* Do you have a vision of yourself in the future? Who do you want to be? How will you get there?
* Keep adding notes to your notebooks.

If you would like a **Secret Garden** Notebook please check out my website www.TriciaFrances.co.uk and if you can send me a photo holding this book I will send you one for free!

As it says in the Workbook:

Now the rest is up to you!

For more clues of what else you might find,

PART 3 THE JOURNEY

the story of what I found in my **Garden** is up next.

With **Secret Garden,** it is important to do the work at the pace of the individual

To acquire a greater understanding of the self

Thought Creates!

PART 3

SECRET GARDEN

THE JOURNEY

For my Angel Cassie & Bear who taught me things I never knew I never knew,
and how to love with all the colours of the wind – dreams do come true,
when you remember how to fly.

Thank you for sharing my journey.

Nyah-Weh-Sgeh-noh.
XX

CONTENTS

SPOILER ALERT

This book gives clues to your own Journey and is best read after completing the Exercises in Part 1 The Workbook

SECRET GARDEN

The Journey

Somewhere in the distance a siren sounded, it was a haunting sound in the still of the night, and something she felt she should be connected with, but she wasn't. She was in dream time, neither awake nor asleep, just a dreamy floating.

Far away she watched the stars twinkle in the evening sky, calling her to join them.

As she drifted, she remembered herself as a little girl, bright and happy. Then manipulation and control had set in, she'd had to escape, somewhere far away that only she knew about, a place where time stood still, a place where there was no time,

Her **Secret Garden**.

And now a long time since her last visit she was here again.

***

Chapter 1

She instantly knew that she was being watched, she raised herself onto one elbow and looked across the lawn. Directly in front of her under the willow was Wolf. She laid back again on the soft grass unafraid. He had always been in her **Garden**, protecting her and teaching her. But today he kept his distance, he knew she needed her space.

He knew what the day had in store for her, more than she did.

She lay quiet for a long time drifting in and out of Dreamtime. She was suddenly aware of someone calling her name.

'Sayana wake up please wake up.'

She sat up with a start, it was her mother, but that was impossible she didn't know about the **Garden**. She looked around but there was no one there except Wolf still sitting under the willow. She waited quietly but the voice had gone.

'I must have been dreaming,' she mused.

She got up and went to sit on her **Seat**. Her very special **Seat** from which she could see the big White House, which she never went into. She could be found there so she always stayed in the **Garden** or her very secret place by the river.

But today she had a problem, she wasn't sure what it was, but she knew that if she ever had a problem and she sat on her **Seat** someone would come by and help her.

Whilst she sat waiting, she looked at her **Garden**. In front of her, the roses bordering the rose **Garden** were as red as ever. She could just make out the maze stretching out beyond them. She felt a sense of yearning as she looked to her right past the river and over to the Sacred Mountains. She had met very special people there, which gave her a sense of wonderment at being alive. She did not know what was to her left, there was a wall and she had never explored this part of her **Garden**, she had never had the time, there was so much to do. She could see the stile which she had climbed over many times to follow the river down towards the Temple of Knowledge.

This was the Kingdom and she had been given the key when she was a child. Then the key had been stolen away with her youth. Her parents had not known what they were doing when they banned her friends and her freedom. She had become empty until now. Suddenly that spark had been ignited and she was back, and things were like they always had been, except she could see white boats on the river, she didn't remember those before, and the **Garden** seemed bigger somehow.

It was curious but apart from the red roses there didn't appear to be any flowers in the **Garden**. She couldn't hear any birds singing either, just an apprehension which hung thickly in the air, like a silent predator waiting for its next meal. But she knew there was ultimately nothing to be afraid of in her **Garden**. Everything here was her dream, she had control to create or destroy anything she wished.

She wondered fleetingly how she had managed to be in her **Garden** at this time when she had virtually forgotten it existed. But she was enjoying it so much that she decided not to analyse but just to flow with it.

She felt a movement at her arm and turned to see a hooded figure standing just behind her.

She jumped, more out of surprise than anything else, she certainly didn't feel afraid.

'My name is Daath. I am your Guide.'

She tried to see his face, but it was hidden by the shadow of his hood.

'I have been instructed to help you decide whether to stay in your **Garden** or to return home. I must warn you that whatever you decide to do will change the course of your life as you have known it. But the choice is yours.

Perhaps you would like to walk for a while?'

Sayana nodded and without a word joined Daath. They walked side by side. Every now and then he would point to bring something to her attention, like a tree or blade of grass and showed her how to merge with the energy of nature's treasures, by breathing them in.

After a while he spoke, his voice rich and resonant.

'It is time to decide. You can either stay forever here meeting with friends in your **Garden**, but there may not be any purpose to your future. I cannot say what lies in that direction. Or you can go back to where you came from this morning. It is possible you could come back to your **Garden**, but the journey here may not be easy. You will have to find your own way next time. The reward for going back is multi-dimensional. You can enrich your existence in a way that you have never imagined. But the chance you take may be to never find your way back here again. The only clue I can give you to decide is this: Whatever you choose will be your own destiny, but one of the ways will lead you to a heightened sense of awareness that you may never experience in the other dimensions.'

Before Sayana could say anything, Daath had vanished.

She walked back to her **Seat** and sat down.

What did all this mean? She had been minding her own business when suddenly she was confronted with decisions. She really did not want to make these decisions. She suddenly felt an urgency that she did not understand. She knew she had to decide. She looked around for Wolf, she had not seen him for a while. She shaded her eyes from the glaring midday sun and peered in front of her to the willow. There he was, not watching her but prowling around, uneasy. He shot her a glance now and again then carried on walking backwards and forwards like the pendulum of a clock.

'Time, yes time' she said. That was the urgency that she felt, she suddenly recognised it, she was running out of time. She had to decide.

She closed her eyes and quietly said ' Help me. I don't know what to do'.

In the stillness the reply came, it was Daath. 'If you go back, you will spend the rest of your life helping others. In return, you can have three things, but you must spend the rest of your life with one foot on the road and the other foot on the pavement. If you don't go back, you can stay here until you feel that you want to leave. But I cannot tell you what is in that future. '

Barely daring to speak Sayana whispered. 'What does that mean – one foot on the road and the other on the pavement?'

'It means that it won't always be an easy journey.'

'Oh. What three things can I have?'

Daath replied, 'Anything you wish'.

'I would like to combine wonderful, inspired music, with writing and working in the Light'.

'You can have those things, my child. What do you want to do?'

'I want to go back'.

In an instant, the **Garden** disappeared.

Chapter 2

The sound of the siren was closer now, and suddenly Sayana felt herself inside the sound. It was all around her, she couldn't work out what was happening, so she opened her eyes. All she could see was the metal roof of some kind of structure above her. She tried to move but her body was stiff, she had awareness but no movement. What had happened to her? She tried to speak but something was on her face. She sensed her surroundings. There was motion so she was in a vehicle, yes suddenly everything added up. It was an ambulance. Then her world went black...

***

She was standing in the doorway of a huge sports hall. There was a red rubber floor with bumps all over it. She was playing with her clackers, those wonderful balls on strings that made a 'clacking' noise when she swung them. There was no one around so she climbed up onto the stage that was situated at one end of the hall. She played for hours, performing in front of her imaginary public. As she jumped and twisted, her beautiful cream and white satin dress swirled with the movement showing her petticoats of white embroidery anglaise. Her red patent shoes taped lightly on the latex floor.

Suddenly she heard voices. She jumped off the stage and went to leave but the voices said,

'Don't go little girl. You are very good at that; we could make you famous. You can have everything that you want. All you have to do is to perform with those things on stage in front of an audience.'

She didn't want to, but they did not listen, she was just a child. They organised a grand event. It seemed just moments until the day came for her to perform, she looked into the audience and there were hundreds of people. As she went on stage everyone clapped but she didn't want to be there, she wanted to be at home, where was her home? She had not been there for a long time. She had been homesick for as long as she could remember. She started the clackers in motion, she performed better than ever before. She felt that if she was good, they would let her go.

Faster and faster the clackers swung, and the audience cheered and shouted for more until exhausted she ran from the stage.

The show was a great success and the people wanted her to be there again, but she did not want to be. She just had to escape, so she ran out of the stadium door.

She ran headlong into an old woman with a stick. The woman was kind to her and asked what was wrong. Sayana started to cry and tearfully told her what had happened. After a long time, she was calmer and asked the old woman to go and play with her.

'I'm sorry my dear I am old, and I cannot play games anymore, but you have your youth and your energy. Play for as long as you can because one day you will end up like me.'

Sayana walked slowly away but turned and looked at the woman with white hair and a bent back.

'Why can't you play? Who are you? How do you know I will end up like you?' she asked in a whisper.

'Because I am you when you get old, don't waste your youth as I did.' Then she was gone.

***

Sayana lay in bed, and as she opened her eyes she saw a young girl, the same young girl, but a bit older, aged about 9. She had bare feet, and her beautiful dress was now in tatters. The clackers were no longer the wonderful gold hearts they had been but were dull and tarnished. Sayana said 'What is wrong? You look so sad.'

The girl did not answer but Sayana instinctively knew this child - it was her. The lifetime of manipulation had led to this, and suddenly Sayana knew that this was something she had to deal with if she was going to stay this time. She would have to work on her life and find out what happened to make her want to leave it.

The child left and as she looked at the light shining through the window. She could see tiny worm-like creatures swimming around in front of her. It was the bacteria in her blood reflecting on her eyes like a giant window into her being. She knew the work that lay in front of her was not only on the physical. She fell into a deep sleep.

Chapter 3

At first, she could not get her bearings. She listened without opening her eyes and all she could hear was the gentle lapping of water and a creaking sound. She lay trying to work out where she was and what had happened before this moment in time. She was being gently rocked and imagined she was on some tranquil sandy beach, with water the colour of sapphires and the sun as bright as the first new penny she had been given as a child.

She opened her eyes, and the sky was clear, except for a few wisps of cloud in the distance. She sat up and realised she was in a small rowing boat moored outside the Temple. She remembered what the boats were for. The legend said that when there were boats on the water in front of the great Temple of Knowledge, there would be ideas and opportunities. Today there were many boats.

She climbed out of the boat and started to walk towards the Temple. She had never been in there before but as she got closer, she felt the excitement start to rise with the anticipation of walking through the door into the unknown.

She reached it and put out her hand and touched the door. It was huge and made from iron-studded wood. Nothing could have penetrated the interior of the Temple unless the door was opened. She took hold of the big black iron ring on the door and with all her strength she began to turn it. Slowly the door opened, and she stepped inside a stone entrance hall. She gasped at the sight in front of her. The hall was a Library filled with books of all colours and sizes, and the shelves stretched upwards, as far as she could see.

Just then a brown-robed hooded figure appeared to her left and motioned for her to follow him. Together they walked down some steps into a long passageway. All along the walls were writings and beautiful drawings. She stared in wonderment as she passed wanting to stop but knowing she had to follow.

Eventually, the passageway opened into a gigantic hall. Everywhere there were huge slabs of stone arranged like shelves. On each slab were bodies, empty of life, and all different ages, shapes, colours, and sizes. Old men and young babies, teenage girls, and middle-aged women.

'What is this place' Sayana asked.

'For many years you have asked why it has taken so long for you to become enlightened. This is the answer. Before you came to this Earth plain you had decided what your age of awareness would be. You chose the lessons you wanted to learn, and you chose the type of body you wanted. This is your blueprint'.

The hooded figure pointed to a female lying on a slab. She appeared to be in her late 30's with red hair and a full figure. Sayana was looking at her double.

'You had to experience the things in your life that you have up till now encountered because you would not otherwise have been prepared for the work ahead.'

Sayana thought back on her life of abuse, manipulation, and co-dependence. She knew they were for a reason but did not understand until now how important each and every event had been in her life.

Sayana looked around. 'Could I have chosen any one of these bodies?'

'Yes!'

'Then why would I want to pick one that is cracking up? she joked.

'Only you can know that' came the reply.

They turned around and the hooded figure lead Sayana out of the Temple. She was desperate to get among the shelves and look through the books, but she was told there would be another time for that. There was much to learn before she would be free to use the Library.

They would come to find her when it was time for her next lesson.

Sayana wandered through the **Garden** following the stream. She had never been this far before and as she walked on, she could hear the sound of the sea in the distance.

After a while up ahead, she saw a cliff and decided to climb it. It was not a difficult climb and as she reached the top she stood absolutely still; awe-struck by the sight in front of her. Slowly she moved forwards and as she stood motionless overwhelmed by the view, she realised that she was looking out from the edge of ever.

Chapter 4

It seemed that she could see forever. There were no limitations to her sight. She looked down and down through the clouds where she could see a beach. In the distance were mountains and streams, forests, and valleys.

A voice by her side made her jump. She turned but there was no one there. She thought the voice had said jump but perhaps she was mistaken. She looked out, again and again, the voice said 'Jump.'

'But it's miles.'

'Don't you trust, do you doubt after all we've shown you? You know you are guided by the Light; you know we would not allow you to come to harm. '

'Who are you?'

'Osiris and I are here to help you. Trust. Jump into the void, leap the vortex, and have faith.'

Sayana looked at the beach far below, somewhere deep inside she knew this was right. She slowly walked to the edge then closed her eyes and stepped off the top of the cliff.

The breeze blew through her hair and pulled at her clothes as she fell, but she was not afraid. Each passing second became more exhilarating, lifting her up and giving her hope until suddenly a huge bird flew around her and as if in slow motion it flew under her, and she landed on its back. He slowed down her descent and she watched in awe as the beach grew nearer. She could see the fish and the coral beneath the water. There was a ship on the horizon, and she could feel the warmth of the sun on her back as they got closer to land. Before long, the bird landed on the beach, and she climbed gently off its back. Before she could turn to thank it, the bird flew away, high into the sky.

For a few moments, she sat on the warm sand and looked out to sea. She reflected on her life and was surprised that she had little knowledge of who she was or where she came from. She knew there were issues that she was working on but felt that the everyday gossip and monkey chatter didn't seem important anymore.

She got up from the sand and decided to explore.

A few yards behind her, to her left there was a **Cave**.

As she entered, she felt the coolness of hundreds of years of peace. The walls were lined with crystal, amethyst, and quartz, glinting in the defused sunlight shining through a hole in the roof. In the centre of the **Cave** was a **Pool** and as she walked towards it she felt the floor vibrate like an ancient heartbeat.

In the corner was a bat. She carefully picked it up and stroked it then put it on a ledge.

She knew this was a message, but she didn't understand what it meant. As she was wondering a voice behind her said

'Hello Sayana. The bat represents Shamanic death, the end of the old life and your identity in that life.'

She turned to see Daath,

'It is also a symbol of rebirth' he continued, 'It is time to let go of all that is outdated and done and to face your fears. As you confront each one it will take you to a higher understanding of the self. Remember that you have full control in your **Garden** and if anything materialises that you do not want here, take it to the entrance of the **Cave** and burn it or throw it into the **Pool** where it will be transmuted into positive energy. Observe what it becomes as there is good in everything.

You do not have to have anything in your **Garden** that you do not wish to have there. Do you have any questions before I leave you to work out the next stage?'

'Yes, how did I get back here? I had made my mind up to go home.'

Daath laughed, 'You are home, Sayana.'

'Oh, you know what I mean! I made the choice but I'm still here.'

'Yes, you did, and it was the right choice, as you see you have been allowed to stay to work things out, which will make your life so different when you finally go back.

But you cannot go just yet, you are still too sick, and it would not be pleasant in that body just now - but if that is what you wish....'

'No no! No, it's OK here right now thanks. Anyway, I'm getting to know my way around. Not many people here though are there. Why is that?'

'One of the things you have chosen in many incarnations was to experience aloneness. Unfortunately, in all your lives except for the first earth life when you were a prophet, you have only experienced loneliness.'

'What is the difference?'

'Aloneness is about being at peace with the self, totally satisfied with your own company and perfectly able to function even in a place where there are no other living beings.'

'Like here.'

'That is your choice. As I have said you can have anything in your **Garden** and as you move forward there will be other beings, not always who you would want, I must warn you! However, as I was saying loneliness is a different thing altogether. It is an emotion unenlightened earth beings feel when they need someone to depend on, even those who have had their awakening will sometimes feel like this because they have not yet dealt with being alone, being self-sufficient, and being satisfied with who they are.

The perfect relationship is between two people who can function quite happily alone forever, if necessary, but when they come together, they create whole people. What you may think of as a super person. If they are perfectly in balance, they will become a boundless creative force. These are the relationships of the future on Earth, super ones!'

Sayana thought about that for a while then asked 'So, explain to me Daath what is this feeling I have of homesickness? I have felt it as long as I can remember, even when I was home with my family?'

'You never knew your family, not your spirit family that is. You were in the care of your Earth parents, and they did the best they could, but they could not give you that understanding, the knowing that comes from the real family. The feeling you have always had that you call homesick is exactly that. But one day when you really know who you are, and you start to meet your fellow travellers the feeling will begin to subside. Then one day you will return to the realms beyond the Earth and the feeling will go forever. It is only felt on Earth because it is the only place where contact with beings in other dimensions is difficult, and sometimes impossible. But tell me, do you have that feeling here in your **Secret Garden**.'

Sayana thought for a few moments and replied with excitement,

'No, do you know Daath I don't. How wonderful to be free from it. I have been so busy exploring that I did not notice. No wonder I have such a sense of freedom!!'

'So are you ready then for your Shamanic initiation?' Daath asked.

'Yep. Whatever comes, as long as it helps.'

'I have a message from Wolf who you must know by now is your Guide and protector. He will not be here at this time because he has faith in you, and he says some things you must do on your own. His message is this:

'When the wind blows you bend but when the hurricane comes you stand strong.'

Do you understand?'

'I think so. What do I have to do?'

'You have done much that is required; you have faced adverse conditions but for the life that is in front of you in the future you will face ridicule when you speak your truth. You have to be strong for this. You have to have 100% faith. We have a great mission for you, and you will not be able to do your work if you do not trust.

So tonight, you have to climb the mountain that you see from the beach. You must climb it alone and in the dark. There will be a place at the top for you to rest and at daybreak you will have to face one of your fears. The way you deal with it is up to you.

In the climb to the top of the mountain, I am afraid you will be given back your human body.'

'Oooww' Sayana exclaimed.

'We cannot make it too easy, or it will be of no benefit to you! Make yourself ready and leave as soon as you can. Goodbye. I will see you again.'

Daath turned to leave, but Sayana caught his arm.

'Daath what if I don't make it? '

'Sayana one thing you must always remember is this. You can only give what you have to give, and you can only do as well as your best. If you do your best whatever the outcome, then you will be satisfied that you could not have done better than you did. Goodbye for now.'

Sayana sat for a moment in the sun outside the **Cave** pondering what to do next. The sun was high in the sky, she had no idea how long this was going to take but she felt she should get herself together soon. She looked about for something to eat or drink, she could feel her human body beginning to take over, the lightness in her step was becoming heavier and she was feeling hot in the midday sun.

She found a water bottle and an old piece of blanket inside the **Cave**. She tucked them under her arm and set off towards the mountain.

***

She reached the mountain by mid-afternoon. Preparing for the climb, she had found a vine and tied the bundle around her waist. She didn't have a knife, but she made a sharp stone by smashing it against a rock. She used it to cut her way through the vines that were matted at the foot of the mountain, prohibiting her progress.

She remembered a spiritual master telling her one day that our journey was like climbing a mountain. At the bottom of the mountain was a burger bar with everything in it that we could ever want for our trip up the mountain. Every now and then on our journey, we would come back down the mountain for a burger and a coke but gradually we came down less and less until one day we would decide never to go back again. Well as there were no hamburger bars she guessed that vines had been used instead to try to fault her journey.

'Huh you won't stop me that easy,' she said in triumph.

There was a clear pathway, although in places it was quite steep and stony, and once or twice she slipped, but generally, the trek was not too difficult. She was about halfway up when the sun started to go down and she guessed she would not reach the top by nightfall.

This concerned her slightly as she had no torch or matches and did not know what was in store at the top. She quickened her speed until she realised that she was in a panic.

She stopped abruptly and sat down.

'This is stupid. If I carry on like this, I shall be exhausted and only just over halfway there. Now let's see what I can do to resolve this.'

She looked about and noticed on the lower levels where she was now that there was a lot of dry cooch grass. She collected a large bundle and tied them with more vines and then collected some suitable stones for making a fire. She resumed her journey, stopping every now and then to collect berries.

Darkness fell and she still had a way to go, so she pushed on, slowly now in case she fell. It was too dark to see clearly but she knew it would be a long fall down the mountain. She started to sing but got too exhausted and thirsty, so stopped for a drink. She heard a movement. It was then that she realised someone was behind her.

'Who's there?'

There was no reply.

'Who is it' she called louder.

Still no reply.

She got up and continued her climb. She moved faster and faster and soon she could make out the ridge at the top of the mountain. She had to get there as quickly as she could, so she made one last effort and panting with sweat she heaved herself on top of the ridge. In front of her was a tipi, but she could feel the presence behind her getting nearer.

She suddenly remembered that everything in the **Garden** was her dream and if she did not want something in it then she could throw it into the **Pool**. But the **Pool** was at the bottom of the mountain.

She did the only thing she knew how and in a clear quiet voice said: 'I love you whoever you are. I welcome you into my presence with all the compassion I have in my being. I send you love.'

Suddenly it was like a fireworks display. Something whizzed skywards and exploded into a million tiny stars.

Sayana laughed and laughed. 'Oh Fear, you can't catch me that easy. I love all beings '

She set down her bundle and struck the stones, which worked instantly with sparks flying onto the dry grass and within a few moments she had a blazing fire.

She peered inside the tipi, and she saw laid out on a beautiful rug was a meal of fruit, nuts, and bread.

She turned and stood outside the tipi, face towards the sky and arms outstretched, and shouted from the mountain top.

'Thank you for bringing me safely this far Great White Spirit. I welcome you into my camp tonight.'

Her voice echoed around, as if nothing else existed in the universe, except for Sayana and her mountain.

But then perhaps nothing else did exist at that moment in time.

Chapter 5

The sun streaming in through the open door flap of the tipi woke Sayana. She went to move and let out a groan.

'Oh, I'm so stiff. It is much easier climbing a mountain out of body rather than in it!

She chuckled and climbed through the flap into the outside world. What a view. She could see her **Garden** and the river and the sea. She had no idea what would happen now that she was here, but she knew she would find out before too long. For now, she decided that she was quite happy to sit and enjoy the peace. Have a little breakfast then go exploring later.

She finished the food that had been left for her last night, then went to lay in the sun.

After a short time, Sayana thought she heard music and sat up. It was drumming and she decided that she would go and have a look. On the other side of the ridge was a dense forest

She left her camp and walked towards it. The music getting gradually louder. She pushed her way through the trees and after a while, she appeared to be in a clearing in the centre. Even though the music seemed to come from here there was not a sign of anyone. But on the other side of the trees was a wooden scaffold-like structure. Sayana walked all around it but could not make out what it was. She decided to climb up it for a better look. There were two narrow planks at either end, and she realised when she got to the top that they were in just the right place for arms and feet.

'Looks like a good place to sunbathe' she said laughingly and spread-eagled across the top. From this vantage point she could see on the other side of the trees was a deep ravine.

She surveyed the scene, and an icy chill touched her heart. There sticking out of the framework of her resting place were native spears. She looked below her and there in all their splendour were rows of Native carved masks, hanging on the structure and in the trees. She had always had a fear of these idols and now she felt she knew why, a past life sacrifice. She panicked and as she tried to get down she knocked one of the masks. As it fell to the floor it revealed what she had always suspected, a shrunken head. There didn't appear to be anyone else around, so she sent a thought out that she definitely did not want any of these artifacts in her **Garden**.

When she got back to ground level, she saw that the structure didn't seem to be fixed into the ground and she assumed it was so that it could be moved into other locations. She tried to push it, but it would not budge, so she looked about and saw a pile of logs on the other side of the clearing. She was suddenly aware that the drumming was getting louder, and she raced across the grass. She felt that time was closing in. She struggled back with the log and wedged over a rock and under the structure. She put all her weight against it, and it began to rock. She kept up the momentum and it gradually started to topple. One last heave and it crashed on its side through the undergrowth and slide down into the ravine. Sayana ran to the edge and watched as it went down and down. She waited for it to hit the water at the bottom, the abyss seemed endless. At last, there was a distant crash as it hit the side then the splintered pieces of wood splashed into the water sending up a spray.

When Sayana walked back into the clearing everything was peaceful, no drumming, no masks, and no shrunken heads. She had cleared this fear forever. She knew it was time to move on.

Chapter 6

Night was drawing in again and the wind had started to howl around the mountain top. The sky was the most brilliant crimson and purple that Sayana felt it was not real. But what was real in this world of Dreamtime or was this all real and the other world an Illusion? She went back inside the tipi and lit the fire. She had found some lighters in the hearth just inside the doorway, so lighting this fire was easier than before. She hoped the tipi was well staked; she didn't fancy being out there tonight.

But she was about to realise that thought creates! There was a sudden whoosh and the stakes lifted and her shelter was carried on the wind down and down the mountain. She was so surprised that she did not catch her blanket as it went flying over her head.

Alone with no protection she wanted to cry but she knew that would not solve anything - but she did it anyway!

'What's going on, Daath can you hear me? Hey, you guys I don't want to be here in the freezing cold with nowhere to go. If this is an initiation, then OK I've got this far - come on give me a break. '

As she sat shivering, she heard a voice booming over the wind.

'Remember. You can do whatever you want, you are the only one that can change your world, no matter what state it is in. Everything was once someone's dream, their highest thoughts, and aspirations, YOU are the result of thought. Thought is law within Earth's universe.

You are afraid of the wind because it is the wind of change. It is blowing away the past and bringing the future. Let go of the fear of change.

All you have to do is think about how you want things to be, and they will BE. Once you understand this, you can change anything.'

The voice was gone. Sayana huddled where the tipi was once warm and cosy. Now it was icy cold, and she felt the wind would blow her over the edge too.

She stood up raised her arms to the cold night sky and shouted,

'OK, you guys up there, listen to this. I don't want a cold bleak life anymore. I want warmth and comfort. I don't want to be on top of a mountain on my own. I want to be with someone who cares, and someone I can care for. I want to be independent but interactive. I don't want to always have to make things good for everyone. I want to let things flow just the way they are.

I DO NOT want to be up on top of this mountain in the freezing cold, I deserve better than that so don't treat me the way I have always treated myself. Have some respect. Wolf this is for you. If you can hear me, I have bent with the wind and now I am standing firm in the hurricane. This is my life and I want to be in control, but you are my Guide and protector and I want you to come and get me NOW '

She let out a howl so loud it cut through the wind. It was returned by another howl and through the shadows she could see Wolf. She ran towards him and for the first time ever he let her climb on his back. She clung to the rich damp fur and together they flew back through time.

Chapter 7

It had been a disappointing wedding. She had wanted more than anything to get married in church, but her parents would not hear of it, she was pregnant, and they were concerned about what the neighbours would say.

She really couldn't give a shit what the neighbours said. She was just glad to finish this part of her life.

At last freedom, OK so she was having a baby but that would not stop her from doing what she wanted. A lifetime of control and manipulation was finally at an end. She was seventeen and her life was in front of her. She didn't hate her parents; they did the best they knew how but they just didn't understand who she was. She felt like her youth had been taken away with her mother's illness and her dad working long hours. When they did have time together at the weekend, Mum would have jobs for him to do so that they could not have fun. Then he would watch TV and they had to be quiet, her sister and her. Her sister was her mothers' favourite and there was no room for Sayana. She knew it did not start that way and she also knew that it happened because she was difficult, but did they know why? Did they know that she was different? That she didn't want to be here, that her life was too painful, that she always felt homesick and could not understand the reason behind it, how could she at that age? Was she adopted or an orphan, surely you can't have these feelings if you actually 'belong 'to a family, she used to think.

She had not been able to talk to them about it and when she tried telling them about her friends, just because they could not see or hear them, they thought she was mad.

So here she was all dressed in white, oh yes, they had agreed to that in the end, and she never did work out that logic, newly married to her ticket to freedom. She did like him, she even thought she loved him, but how could she when she did not love herself.

The honeymoon lasted a few months then the bills and the damp cold flat started to open her eyes. She was still in the same situation, only now it was worse. At least her Mother had cooked and cleaned now she had to do it, she had to do everything. He was useless. She remembered the day he nearly blew himself up trying to put a plug on the TV.

She remembered thinking 6 years and 3 babies later that nothing had changed except for the surroundings. Manipulated by his insecurity and the defencelessness of her children. So, after another 4 years, she found someone else to take her away from it all and give her that freedom. Only this time he kept her down by hitting her and abusing her children. Her life went from bad to worse.

She put up with the beatings, adultery, manipulation, and degradation because she did not respect herself, and she did not know there was any other way. She felt this must be what she deserved.

She stood in the doorway with Wolf, looking at her children. They were women now. They too had learnt how to manipulate her, to get what they wanted, because she was afraid of being on her own. That was it. That was what she had come into this life for. What did Daath say 'Aloneness is not the same thing as Loneliness.' Ah, so that is why I was manipulated. I came in with the fear of being alone. Wolf, I understand it all. YES, We can go now,' She had a feeling of jubilation and shouted, 'I understand!'

Chapter 8

Sayana was sitting on the grass in her **Garden**. It was the following afternoon, and she was talking to Wolf as she stroked his fur.

'Why did I have to come to Dreamtime before I could understand what was wrong with my life? I suppose I am lucky really. I bet not everyone has this chance. They just die.'

Just then Daath appeared. He came and sat down with them on the grass.

'Who are you Daath?'

'Don't you know?'

'No, If I did, I wouldn't ask would I?'

'No, I suppose you wouldn't. Some people call me Death. I am the bringer of souls. You see there is no such thing as death, it is just a transition from one dimension to the next. On earth, your physical bodies only have a certain life span. Your spirit can never die so I help beings to become in tune with their soul so that they can move on quickly to their next incarnation. I am also known as The Light. All creation occurs through me. I am the doorway to the tree of knowledge. Before you can walk through the doorway, you have to know where it is. You found yours in your **Garden**: Sometimes symbolized as the Tree of Life, sometimes seen as a doorway.'

'How much longer do we have on earth? '

'It depends on what you mean by we. If you mean yourself personally, that is up to you. Right now, you have a choice. If you mean we collectively, there is also a choice but on a higher level of consciousness. All I can tell you is that the People have 12 years to put it right, till the year 2007*. Things are changing fast, and it will never be the same after that.'

'You must have seen many wonderful things Tell me about your work.'

'It is of little importance to you. Your own **Secret Garden** adventure is truly amazing, as is everyone's, but it is only important to that individual. However, I will tell you a story.

Once upon a time, there were three nomads. They were very ugly indeed. They wandered the earth searching for the Holy Grail. They had heard it was from other worlds. They came upon a **Pool** of crystal water and as they looked into the **Pool** their reflections jumped out and disappeared.'

Daath took a deep breath and laid back on the grass. Sayana sat with expectation, but nothing happened.

'OK Daath so tell me the rest.'

'The rest Sayana is for you to write. When you have the rest, you will know how to find the holy grail, and how to find your soul. No one can do that for you. All we can ever do is show you how to get the keys to your kingdom. The rest is up to you.'

They both sat in the sun, not speaking until eventually Daath got up waved goodbye and walked away.

'I wish he wouldn't do that,' Sayana said half to herself and half to Wolf.

*(**Author Note**. 2007 was a landmark year in technology. Internet and social media were evolving. On 29/6/07 the first iPhone was released – a computer in the hand.)

'So why would the reflections jump out? Let's go to the river and see.'

They walked across the field and climbed over the stile that led to the river. When they reached it, she sat down, and Wolf sat beside her.

She peered in.

'OK, so what can I see? Myself. Right, so the first thing they must have seen was themselves. Now Daath said they were ugly. So maybe that is why the reflections jumped out. No that's too easy. There must be more to it than that. Maybe they disappeared too, you can't have a reflection if you don't have a body.'

Sayana saw the funny side of this and jigged around singing 'I ain't got no body' for a few moments. She wondered if maybe they were in Dreamtime where anything was possible. But she knew Daath would have told her if that was the case.

Back to the drawing board. What else is there around. The trees, the flowers, the birds. Those reflections are still there.

'THAT'S IT.' She squealed, 'The reflections jumped out because they were not loved. The nomads only ever saw the beauty in others and their surroundings and not in themselves. To find the Grail we must love ourselves and look into our own hearts for the pure unconditional love that the Grail provides. When we love ourselves the love that we give is magnified. And because everything is a reflection it becomes an ever-overflowing cup.'

'But remember we cannot help those that do not help themselves. All we can offer them is our support. We do not have the right to try to change another's life only give them a guiding hand when they ask for it. You are doing very well Sayana; I am proud of you. '

'Oh, Daath you made ME jump. Well, what happens next?'

'I want you to meet Oleron. He will be your Guide now. You cannot learn from just one person, and you are slowly getting well, I see my work is nearly done.'

'No, you can't go, I have too many questions. '

'You will be able to ask Oleron. '

From behind the Temple Sayana saw a young man in a white robe walking towards them. He had thick golden hair that almost touched his waist. He greeted them with a smile.

Daath took Sayana's hand and said,

'May the force be with you.'

In the next moment, he was gone.

They stood in silence for a while then Oleron spoke quietly. His voice sounded like delicate wind chimes full of harmonics and sunshine.

'Hello Sayana, I am Oleron. I have come from the celestial realms to help you grow. We have watched your progress and we are very proud of you. We see things from a different perspective than the way you do on Earth.

Look into your heart and see what is really there. The material is only a manifestation of thought as you know it. You also know that you cannot bring material things here with you, just the knowledge of who you are or were. You have felt great loss over the past few years when people have not understood you and relationships have not worked out.

Sometimes a person cannot work at your speed so let them be with love, cherish what they are and allow them to grow in their time. You know this anyway and you are working hard on yourself. Never forget the **Secret Garden** again. When you go, tell others about it. It is a place where individuals can grow at their own speed. By facing things from the past, present, and future they can be in control of their life, enriching it changing it and eliminating things which are no longer needed.

You have passed the initiation, you have chosen what you want, or rather what you don't want in this life.'

Oleron sat on the grass and Sayana joined him. Wolf went back to the willow and watched as Oleron started to speak.

'In the beginning, The Creator, which some people know as God, created the world through combined thought and all things in it from its own image. It was indeed a truly wonderful magician to create a world of such beauty. It showed a loving heart and a beautiful mind. It was like all the aspects of beings coming together. One universal Creator. But it has not manifested as in the original Vision because all minds have dark places, thoughts that can manifest into reality. They became monsters from the mind; dinosaurs, volcanoes, and earthquakes, are just examples. They can be turned into positivity unless you give your power to someone else. Then it can become corrupt. Man was created in love but took too much control. All you can do is live in the Light. Appreciate all things whether you think they are right or wrong because they are all other people's truths. They may not be yours, but they are part of this intricate interdimensional web and before too long it will be the Great Creator and Mother Earth that will restore the balance.

Even in the infinite wisdom of creation, the black side has to be faced and included, because you cannot have one without the other, they are counterparts.

Be assured everything is going according to plan - maybe not the plan that the lighter ones wanted originally! It is about balance, as above so below. There really is no good and evil, just different aspects of the whole.'

Oleron took a scroll of paper from his pocket. As Sayana looked, the words on the paper came to life.

'This paper is a copy taken from the book L'Oriel, which you will find in the Living Library in the Temple of Wisdom. I would like to read it to you if you would allow.'

'Oh yes please, it looks so interesting.'

'L'Oriel means ' *The projecting window of upper storey.'* - meaning a higher view.

In the beginning, when time did not exist there was a void. It was filled with nothing but nothing was everywhere.

To the seer, it was not a black hole but a wonderous place of sound and light.

Colours were beyond belief and the feeling of weightlessness was overwhelming.

A great peace touched all those that experienced the void.

Q. So what happened to it?

A. Oh it still exists in the realms of the universe, but some minds do not accept its existence and for them it has vanished.

Q. What is the object of the void?

A. We talk about object with different meanings.

Q Purpose?

A The purpose of the void is to be still in solitude to reflect without reflection, to experience without experience, to do nothing without something - just to be.

Find that quiet time in your own universe and all will become clear.

Cherish the light and sound in your world. Enjoy all experiences. This is the best adventure yet. Every adventure has its meaning, and each becomes clearer and more exciting.

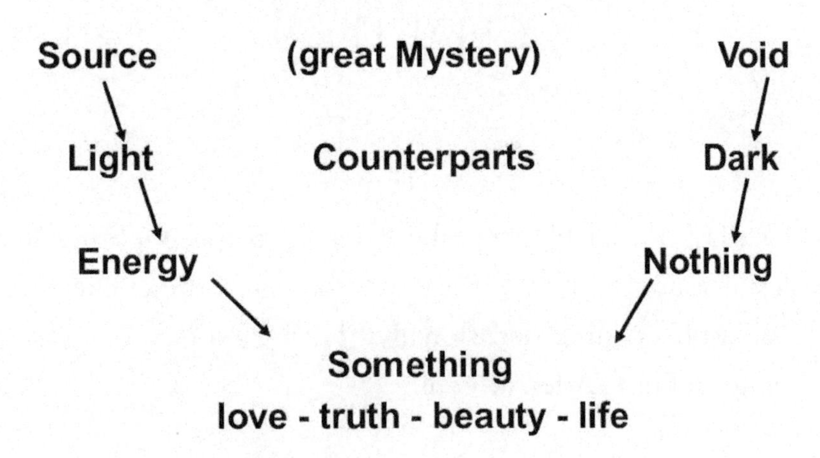

There is Balance in everything

Sayana looked at the page in wonderment as the words danced with light.

'You have done much today. It is time for rest. Tomorrow you can explore your **Garden** peacefully on your own. I bid you good night.'

Oleron got up, bowed, handed Sayana her blanket, and turned to go back the way he came.

CHAPTER 9

As Sayana lay on her blanket, she listened to the Nightingale singing. Such a wonderful sound even at night-time. She heard the crickets chirruping around her and Wolf howling occasionally. Then a sudden thought occurred to her. She had other beings in her **Garden** after all.

***

She awoke early, she wanted to make the most of this day and explore as far as possible.

She walked to the stream to wash then she picked fruit for her breakfast. She was full of excitement knowing today would be an adventure.

She walked back to the **Seat** and sat for a while looking out over her **Garden**. There didn't seem to be barriers anywhere, the wall had disappeared. There were a few places that seemed to contain nothing at all, just a void. But the trees around her were green and the sound of the river was pleasing in the background. Sayana looked to her left and saw a place that she had not noticed before. She walked over and saw that there were three steps leading to a bog. It was full of rubbish. As she stood wondering how it had got there, she realised it represented the rubbish in her life. She stepped down into the stinking sludge careful to avoid all the junk.

As she walked, she trod on something hard. She bent down and picked up a sling shot, and a branch which was next to it. A few steps further along she saw something shining. She picked it up and after a bit of polishing realised that it was a coin.

A voice in her head said there are treasures in the dross, you just need to recognise them. Everything has a purpose.'

Sayana tucked the three objects into her belt and carried on walking through the mud. After a while, she tripped over something. When she looked it was a small container. She opened it and smelt the contents. It smelt like detergent.

'I love my **Garden**, and this is spoiling it. Maybe I can get rid of this muck,' she almost laughed at the thought of such a small container doing such a big job!

Nevertheless, she took off the lid and sprayed it over the bog. To her amazement, the sludge started to dissolve.

As she held up the container to the sun in thanks she noticed some writing on the glass:

Ingredients; LOVE, PEACE, & HARMONY.

She suddenly realised that this was how to change things in her life and her **Garden** - with love.

She walked on a little further and found a handle sticking out of the bog. She pulled it and discovered it belonged to a leather bag. On opening it she found it was full of documents. She walked back to the steps and sat down and opened the leather bag. She pulled out the papers. They were in note form, and it was her handwriting:

1) 3/5/95 Loving another

Sometimes hearts are like safes. When you open the combination and look inside it might appear empty but right at the back in the corner you will see a tiny light. On inspection, you will see this is actually a tiny red heart. Expand the light and then love will grow. Creep into a person's life slowly, into their hearts. Gently not blasting. Help them to feel secure, show them love, and give them time.

2) Abundance

Know you are good enough and that you deserve goodness in your life.

3) How to win

Eat sleep and work to proportion, never be in 'Want.'

Have what you need. Move any surplus around so that it gets used beneficially. Holding on causes blocks.

4) How to love your partner

Give them freedom and let them grow, be secure, sincere and trust. Doubt and it will creep in. Too much work takes away the fun. Be organised and things will run smoothly.

5) Miracles

Never doubt miracles. The key is to trust. But be aware of power, as without compassion miracles are useless.

6) Life's journey

The train of life picks you up and puts you down where ever you decide to stop until one day you will reach the end of this journey.

Highly evolved souls had to experience life on Earth first. There are no short cuts, just short lives.

MEDITATION

Colour and Aura

Go into your **Secret Garden** and ask for three colours to work with. They will be given as ribbons, butterfly wings, strips of paper or the like. The first colour represents your soul colour - the one we vibrate with. The second one will be what you are lacking and the third will be what you have an excess of right now.

***

Sayana closed her eyes and sat for a moment contemplating, then put the papers back into the bag. She laid it by her side on the step and then scanned the bog. Not too far away she saw another handle sticking up through the dissolving mire. She jumped down and walked over to it. This one was on a door that opened like a hatch.

Sayana stepped inside and she could not believe her eyes. This was paradise. Vines wound themselves around the mangoes in the sun, and beautiful birds sang and flew from tree to tree. Wonderful flowers bloomed in all the colours of the rainbow. Lush and green, this was Sayana's inner **Garden**, not managed and neatly kept like the **Garden** above, but natural and free. This was the doorway to her soul.

Sayana stayed in the paradise **Garden** for some time, touching the trees and the flowers and watching the butterflies flit from one to the next. She realised what beauty could come from within, despite all the negativity that seemed to stick on the surface.

Eventually, she decided to climb back into her **Garden**, she realised that if she stayed where she was, she would not be able to accomplish what she had come to do.

As she surfaced, she looked about and was amazed to see the sludge was almost dried up now. There were even weeds growing out of it. There were many more coins, now shining where the mire had been, also rose trees and large crystals.
'Do you see now Sayana that there is treasure in the mire? The problems in life bring forth the greatest gifts.'

Sayana turned and in front of her stood the most beautiful being. Almost in a whisper she said, 'Who are you?'

'I am Osiris.'

He took her gently by the hand and led her back to the step and sat down next to her.

'Sayana, do you see the beauty growing through the bog? You found your **Garden** of Eden, the inner place. This was where the monsters were kept but you sent out love and they dissolved.

Look Sayana the **Garden** of Eden is growing out of the bog.'

Sayana watched in wonderment as the most beautiful trees and flowers came into view.

Osiris and Sayana sat for a while and then he left saying he would see her again.

Chapter 10

The day was not sunny as previously and as Sayana was preparing her fruit for breakfast, she sensed someone behind her. As she turned, she was overwhelmed by the beauty of the being in front of her. She was dressed in a purple robe and spoke gently.

'Hello Sayana. I am Sarah, the time has come for you to enter the Temple of Wisdom and Knowledge. Today will be a great day. You will receive the keys. You will be able to enter the Temple whenever you wish and see wonderful things. It is where the living Library is stored, some know it as the Akashic records. Here you can learn everything from the beginning of time. Please eat then we can start our journey.'

As Sayana ate her food she listened to Sarah, her words hanging on the air like morning dew, crisp and clean. She told her that she would meet her other animal **Guides**, one of which was only available to those that were on their path.

When she had finished eating, they crossed the lawn to the gate which led down to the river. As they crossed the stile Sayana saw something move. She climbed over and peered around a bush.

'Quick Sarah look at this. It's a pure white cow.'

Sarah's laugh echoed like wind chimes across the valley.

'Sayana that is no cow, it is a white buffalo, indeed an honour to be your Guide!'

Embarrassed, Sayana curtsied in front of White Buffalo.

'I'm terribly sorry, please excuse my ignorance. Thank you for not running away' White Buffalo nudged her gently then stood very still.

'She wants you to climb on her back.'

Sayana did as she was told, and they headed down river to the Temple.

'Do you see the boats, Sayana? They are opportunities. When you see new ones as you do now this means that many new ideas are coming. If they are broken and wrecked it is a sign that you are not making the most of them or worse still you have missed them along the way. Always watch this, as it is a guide to your progress.'

They reached the steps of the Temple and Sayana climbed down from White Buffalo's back and together she and Sarah walked into the Temple.

She led her down into the basement and along the way explained many symbols and pictures that were painted on the walls.

'We must be quiet now there is a lesson in progress. Would you like to listen, it is about Karma'?

'Yes please.'

They quietly entered a great hall, with many pillars. They sat at the back and listened to a brown-robed monk giving the lecture.

'Why are there no people here,' she whispered.

'Because this lecture is being given to the higher self of many people. They don't have to be here; it touches them in meditation and Dreamtime. Sshh now please.'

KARMA

Today's lesson is about Karma.

Karma is a physical action, the law of cause and effect, or ethical causation. Karma can affect not only people but the planet also. The following is from a volume in the Library, entitled:

A QUESTION OF KARMA

By now I would imagine that the majority of people reading this are aware that something drastic is happening to our planet, but many won't understand the enormity of it.

We are all moving forward at our own speed to personal and planetary awareness. Some people will have traumatic or Near Death Experiences (NDE) to allow this process to take place.

We are becoming more aware of our gifts and using them to help others, we are finally finding our way onto our spiritual and life paths.

In 1991 I had an NDE through a serious illness and I knew that if I came back my life would be dedicated to helping others to find their true potential.

I always tell people that the hardest thing is to really look at themselves. Once we have overcome that hurdle we can start to do that work. People take varying degrees of time to deal with this issue, depending on the Karma that they must deal with, and whether it is from this life or some past existence.

Often people ask me to help them find out about their past lives, but this is only necessary if there is still an unresolved issue. Say you had a past life where you were burnt alive, but you had gone on to deal with this issue in a subsequent life, then there is no point in reliving the trauma of this horrific death. But say you suffered from chronic claustrophobia in this life then it would be of value to explore the possibilities of unfinished business from the past. It could well be to do with the fact that you may have got shut into a cupboard at the age of 2 or 3 in this life!

Everything we do, every action against our own self and others is registered into our being. If we try to live a good and compassionate life, we will build more positive karma than if we spend it being aggressive and unemotional towards others. Every time someone treats us well or badly it affects our karma. Sometimes causing disease of the physical body or mind. It is a well-known fact that stress can cause serious illness. Stress is caused by situations that happen outside our physical body: an argument with a loved one, victimisation at work or school etc. that then filters into our physical and mental being and become contributors to sickness.

Now picture the Earth as we know it today, and how we really feel about it. When we get up in the morning, we put our feet on its safe predictable crust, in fact when we sleep at night we are lying on it, totally supported whilst we dream.

But is it so stable?

Since the beginning of time every time an action takes place, we are infusing the Earth's Karma with our own. Each war or disaster brings fear and pain, each celebration brings laughter. Everything has its effect, from a tiny ant to the strongest man. But the trauma of explosion and exploitation has taken its toll.

Imagine again, if you were continually confused by the people around you, first making love, then blowing each other up and every time they came to you for comfort. Then they polluted the air around you by continually spraying aerosol cans and smoking, then feeding you with toxic substances, if you were lucky, you would have a physical or mental breakdown, if you were unlucky, you would face death.

Well, that is where Mother Earth is right now. Years of abuse has taken its toll; she is heading for a breakdown. Simple to understand if you look at it with this view, isn't it?

The world that we feel safe on is like a huge aircraft, once it runs out of fuel it will crash.

We are having more natural disasters than ever before, quakes, volcanoes, lightning storms, floods, fires, and so the list goes on.

But how can we stop this from happening?

By becoming more in tune with ourselves and the planet. As we heal ourselves, we heal the world.

I teach groups of people how to scan their bodies for energy blocks and then how to set about the healing process.

What if we were to do this with the Earth?

What if we were to stop throwing toxic rubbish into holes we have dug in her 'body'?

What if we were to start to put back what we have taken away?

What if we were to cleanse her atmosphere so that she can breathe? If we treated another human being the barbaric way we treat the Earth we would surely kill them.

What happens to a person who is on the verge of a physical or mental breakdown? They become unpredictable. What if you stepped out of bed tomorrow morning and there was nothing there? This is a real possibility. The earth's plates are moving causing structural problems within the Earth, who knows what might happen tomorrow morning if we don't stop fighting each other and concentrate on the real problem. There will be little point in wars if we have nothing to fight for.

I feel we have only a short time to turn things around before this Earth has changed forever. We don't have to turn into hippies to make peace in the world, all we must do is care.

Instead of spending 100% of your time in the material rat race, take time to stop and walk by the river or in the forest. Breath in the fresh air and feel the energy from nature. Don't just look at what is around you, really see.

And do you know something? It won't cost you a penny!!

Our inner journey moves on and as it does, we find a Freedom that up till now was an elusive dream. By letting go of negative situations and past Karma we can gain this Freedom more quickly.

It is a good idea to release negative Karma with everyone we know or have known.

Karma is created by actions and thought forms in this and past lives.

To be able to give this life our best shot it is very important that we clear any negative Karma.

Here is how to release negative Karma:

Relax deeply.

See yourself standing in a void, and from above a golden ray is shining down through your Crown Chakra which is on the top of your head. The golden ray flows through your body, and out through your feet to the ground. As you watch it, it shines from within into your aura, which is on the outside of your body. If there are any dark places in your aura fill them with a golden star and as the star bursts it takes away the dark negative areas. When your aura is clear and full of golden light try to push it out as far as possible. When you feel it is as large as you can make it, bring the golden light back inside, leaving all negativity as far outside your aura as you can. You now have the golden light inside you. Walk a few paces and you will see a **Waterfall** made from silver rain or tiny silver stars. Go and stand under this **Waterfall** and as it washes over you, feel it cleansing your etheric body. Walk further into the **Waterfall** and you find yourself inside a huge **Cave**. This is where you have stored situations from your past. Things that have been too painful to deal with.

You know you must enter this **Cave**, but before you do, see yourself surrounded by your golden light. If you feel more comfortable put on your Light body of pure white Light.

Now enter the **Cave**. There is nothing there that can do you harm, they are just memories which you have hung onto over the years. When you are ready walk forward.

What do you see around you?

You are going to ask for the help of the **Waterfall** to wash these memories away. As each negative thought or action comes towards you send it to the light to transmute it into positive energy. Any stubborn links with the past can be thrown into the **Waterfall** where they will be stripped of any darkness and dissolve.

Now that you have got rid of a lot of the rubbish, you may want to work on people that are causing you problems. These problems can be from this life or a past encounter.

Sometimes people will not want to accept your love, so leave them that day and try again tomorrow. If you are honest with this visualisation, you will eventually be able to let them go. If then you are truly meant to be together, they will come back into your life with a richer, more loving relationship, that gives each of you the space you need to do your work. Alternatively, if this ends your relationship in this life then you can know that you have released your negative Karma and once again you will be free to do your work. Be strong as this is a necessary act for any Lightworker or seeker of a better life.

How to release negative Karma with people.

You can work on up to three people at a time if they are linked in some way. It is also a good idea to do it with your own spirit as it clears any negative thoughts you have about yourself.

Go back and stand in front of the **Waterfall** where you came into the **Cave**. Look ahead, can you see a **Pool**? This works like the **Waterfall** and might be easier to use with people.

Visualise the person or people in question standing in a row in front of you by the **Pool**. As you stand in front of them, working with one at a time, you open your heart and send a burst of white light of unconditional love from your heart into theirs 3 times for 5 seconds. Then close the heart chakra, give this person a hug and let them go on their way. Walk to the next person. Repeat this until you have sent love to each one. Remember the pain of release is only a moment in time and ultimately only good can come from it. .... This exercise can take up to 3 months, but you will know when it is complete because they will become invisible, and your spirits will merge.

If this becomes difficult with anyone throw them into your **Pool**!

Negativity will be released and float upwards towards a gap in the top of the **Cave** where it will transmute into positive energy in the form of butterflies, stars light or other such things.

There was silence for a few moments then in a whisper the monk turned the page and continued:

TREES

Growing ever skywards,
like the mighty oak that sheds its leaves,
we must let go of redundant situations
and emotions that are spent.
Every winter has a spring
when the leaves will grow again.
Why hang on to things that are dead.
Let go and bloom once again.

You have made positive steps today to a happier, healthier life free from negative ties.'

The monk closed the book, placed it on the table then after dismissing the class, left the hall by a door at the far end.

'Sarah. The part about the NDE was about my life,' Sayana whispered.

Sarah smiled, 'You could go and look at the book.'

Sayana walked across the hall and picked up the book. She stood in disbelief.

'What does it say' asked Sarah.

'It is by me, with a mention to my friends on the front page. Hey, it is written in 1996, but it's only 1991'.

'Yes Sayana, you will **write that book**. Remember there is no time. The past, future and present are all one. You are at this moment standing in the here and now, but that is when you want it to be. The books in the Library reflect information from all time.

From the moment you **write that book,** you will be writing your future. You will have got to a point in this incarnation where you will have freedom and control. The book is about your growth. Remember we can write our own lives, but many give control over to others and spend the rest of their life complaining about how badly they are being treated. If they moved and respected themselves, they would not be treated that way.

You have learnt much today. It is time for me to leave. But you can come and look at the books in the Library whenever you choose. There is much to learn!!'

By this time they had walked back to the heavily carved wooden door and as she opened it, much easier now, they could see it was raining.

'You remember the bush where you first saw White Buffalo. Look there you may find somewhere dry to shelter.'

Sayana bid Sarah farewell then watched the rain for a while. It was a bit chilly too so she decided to have a look where Sarah suggested, she thought sleeping out tonight would not be desirable. So, she hurried back up to the gate and rounded the bushes. The sight before her gave her such a surprise that she let out a yell.

The most beautiful building stood in front of her. It had dozens of tiny panes of glass, like the many facets of a crystal. It was like a summer house, but much more beautiful. Passion flowers and jasmine were climbing over part of the roof. Sayana opened the door and stepped inside. The room was bare except for a large cane couch which was suspended somehow from the roof. It was full of comfortable cushions and blankets. It overlooked the river and when Sayana sat on it, she could see as far one way as the Temple, at the base of the river, and as far as the cliff the other way, which lead to the sea, and in the distance, she could see the Sacred mountains.

'What a wondrous place this is. I am going to watch the river and ponder on the day's events. She made herself comfortable but before she could do anything else, sleep crept up and took her away to Dreamtime.

In her dream, Sayana was lying on the cane couch, and she saw a scorpion on the floor. She watched it and as it moved, she was aware her body was not as before. Her legs were long and slender, and she realised she was in the body of a mantis. She stepped gracefully down from the couch on the other side to the scorpion. It was like they were dancing, keeping their distance, warily circling around and never losing sight of each other. Gradually she and the scorpion transformed back into their human bodies. He was a man she did not recognise at first, although she felt she knew him. She was overwhelmed with love but realised how dangerous the game could become.

Chapter 11

Sayana had many experiences in the Temple. She loved to dance under the skylight in the sun. She found that if she stood on the sundial she would get answers relating to time. One day when she did this the dial pointed to a time. When she asked what this meant she was told that this is where she was in her life. As the days moved on so did her time. It did not relate to minutes and hours but to how much she had learnt - at this point she was halfway there. She asked about others, but she became increasingly uneasy and realised that she was accessing private sacred information and she asked it to stop and not to enlighten her regarding other people's journeys.

She often sat at the table under the skylight reading a book from the shelves that went up for miles. Once or twice, she climbed the spiral staircase to see if she could get a book off the top shelf. Floors, and floors she climbed but eventually she would lie down and go to sleep knowing that she was between layers of living history, past future and present.

She was thankful for the keys to the Temple for here she had learnt many things.

Chapter 12

Sayana woke to the sound of drums. She had been sleeping under the willow. She looked around for the source of the sound and to one side of the **Garden** she saw a Native American playing a drum and singing. Like her, his age was difficult to determine, his skin was light tan, and his hair was shaven at the sides with feathers and beads woven into the remainder. He wore fringed white hide breeches and had tattoos on his arms and shoulders. She sat watching him and listening to the hypnotic beat of his drum. After some time, she got up and went and sat in front of him. He did not look up but kept his eyes closed swaying to the rhythm of the music.

She started to sing with him, and he abruptly stopped, suddenly aware of her presence.

'Hello. My name is Sayana. What are you doing in my **Garden**?'

'My name is Bear, and I am your brother. Do you not remember me?'

Sayana looked into his eyes and a familiarity started to grow inside her. She tried to remember, and then Bear spoke again.

'Do you not remember our Mother died and you looked after me?

A memory stirred and Sayana closed her eyes and travelled back in time along the threads of her mind. She saw them both sitting by the river watching the fish dart back and forth.

'Yes, I remember. Why are you here?'

'To help you to remember this piece of your past. It is important that you go back with all the information there is. I'm here to remind you of the love in that life, the closeness between us, and the fun we had.'

Without taking his eyes off her he started to drum, quietly at first, the rhythm like a heartbeat.

She felt herself being pulled into his eyes' the windows of his soul, deep deep into unending love. Round and round she twisted, back, back through time….

She sat in front of the tipi; it was covered in the most wonderful paintings. She had never seen such colours. Her mother had painted it, she was so good, even as a child, so her father had called her "Little painted feather," a name which has stayed with her throughout her life.

She loved her little brother, and she would sing to him, soothing him to sleep. She remembered the song and started to sing.

Oh, Wey Oh Wey Oh
we're walking through time with our hearts in our hands,
Oh, wey Oh wey Oh
we're walking through time with our hearts in our hands.

Through her thoughts, filtered the heartbeat of the drum. She opened her eyes and there in front of her was her brother, but he was a man now.

'How did you get into my **Garden**? How can you be here when I had forgotten? I thought I could only have the things I want. How can I want you if I don't remember you?'

'Sayana, don't you know anything about your higher self. Don't you know that we are all connected somewhere outside our conscious mind?

As he spoke the sound of the drum was getting louder, the beat faster, she felt her head swimming again, she felt those soft eyes watching her pulling her in.

Back, back..........remembering.

***

And now here he was sitting in front of her. He looked different now, that is why she had not recognised him. He was the native man he had wanted to be.

He was known as Satanta, the Orator of the Plains, because of his speeches. When the buffalo were killed, he said 'Has the white man become a child, that he should recklessly kill and not eat? When the red man slays game, they do so that they may eat and not starve.'

But how could he be here now?

Sayana heard the beat of Bears drum bringing her back to **Garden**.

'I heard your thoughts, little sister. I am here in your **Garden** in another life, and I will be in your future in yet another, like the strands of a cobweb we weave lives together, changing, and adding all the time. How does that life relate to the one you are in outside your **Garden**? Close your eyes and watch the tapestry of life weave its living canvas.'

Bear started to drum quietly again.

***

Sayana thought about the last few years. They had all come for her wisdom, all her brothers, drawn from miles away in incredible twists of fate.

But then she met Bear, the one she had been waiting for - her blood brother. He had touched her life 11 years before, but she did not know about such things then.

And through the strangest circumstances he came again. He came back time and time again for her wisdom. Her knowing angered him; his reflection angered him more. But he kept coming back.

But she knew they had to do their own work and she could not carry him like a big sister anymore. So how could she help him this time?

By waiting and giving him the space to do as he will.

The drumming got louder, and Bear said ' The Great Chief Washakie from the Shoshoni's said ' When favour is given to the white man, he feels it in his head and his tongue speaks. When kindness is shown to an Indian, he feels it in his heart and his heart has no tongue'. Then the tears fell from his eyes – the eyes are the windows of the soul!'

As Sayana watched her brother was also crying.

***

A little later they were sitting by the fire.

'Why do the Indians come into my **Garden**, into my life? Since I was a child, they have been there.?'

'They have been teaching you about the ways of the Earth, preparing you for your mission, since you came onto your Earth walk.

You helped and cared for me in that life, and I am here to do the same for you in this life, if you will let me.'

'Oh Yes Bear, I accept your help, no matter how hard I have to look at myself. Thank you for being here.'

They sang and drummed till it was dark and Sayana fell into a happy contented sleep.

Chapter 13

The sun was shining brightly when Sayana awoke. She picked berries for her nourishment and drank water from the clear stream. She walked towards the river but just as she was about to pass through the gate something caught her eye through the mighty weeping willow. As she watched she felt someone beside her. It was Bear. Without a word, he motioned her to follow him. They walked forwards past the weeping willow, and she found herself at the top of the mountain and in front of her, seated silently around in a circle, were eleven elders.

Bear gently sat her in the centre of the circle and took his place with the rest. Sayana felt uncomfortable and stood up and tried to sit next to him, but he stood again and took her back to the centre. The circle of twelve started to sing and she became more and more uncomfortable. She felt that the layers of her being were stripped away, leaving her exposed and raw. She wanted to run and cry, she wanted to leave but she knew that she would have to go through this again. So, she stayed. She stayed and cried. She stayed and let the layers of her being fall away. She knew many things, more than when she had walked into the circle, but she knew that there were many more to learn. She tried to remember what she had learnt but she couldn't find any words, just a knowing that she had changed. Bear held her with his gaze, supporting and encouraging her to let go and be at peace. She wanted to run to him, to be in his arms and tell him that she never wanted to be alone again, but she knew that now was not the time. Whatever it was that she had to find beneath the layers would not be there today or tomorrow but sometime in the future, only then could she tell him how she felt. Because then in this life he would be someone other than her brother. For now, he was her Guide as she had been his all those years before when they were children.

She felt herself slipping into Dreamtime.

***

Sayana was standing in the **Cave**; it was dark apart from the light that was above and around and inside her. As she moved the light moved with her. She walked forwards and a huge crystal came into view. She walked up to it and tried to see her reflection, but the facets were cloudy. She tried to polish the facet nearest her with her hand, but it was very difficult, and it had sharp edges.

So, she tore a strip of fabric from the hem of her dress and walked to the **Pool** just beside her and dipped the cloth into the crystal-clear water. Then she dabbed the cloth into the sand on the floor of the **Cave** and proceeded to rub the sharp edges of the crystal with the sharp sand. Slowly it began to smooth down. Sayana then went back to the **Pool** and washed away the sand. She took the clean cloth back to the crystal and began to polish it. As she did the light began to stream into the **Cave**, sending rainbows from the crystal across the walls.

The facet was in the area of emotions, and she realised how in the past she had taken away her loved one's independence by caring for them too much. She realised it was because she needed to be cared for herself. But she had not been able to express that feeling and so had taken away the chance of love by overwhelming others.

As she polished, the crystal showed her a vision.

She saw Wolf who had always been there, unobtrusively protecting her. Buffalo waited quietly for Sayana to climb on her back. The boats on the river were opportunities just floating silently waiting for the time when Sayana would climb aboard of her own free will.

From inside the crystal, a voice spoke.

'Some people help too much; they do not see it from other perspectives. They are single-minded and want to help but helping is only useful if the receiver wants to be helped. There are times in a person's life when help is detrimental because they must do it for themselves - or not!

You can offer help and if it is uncomfortable for either of you then do not get hurt if the offer is declined.

Sayana, you have begun to see the thread of it. Follow along to the end and see where it goes. See if you want to pick up all the conditions it brings along the way. When you can do this, you have truly begun to learn. You will understand it from the other side also. - Reflections!!

You often wonder about unconditional love. That is not putting up with whatever anyone chooses to throw at you. Unconditional is giving without requiring a return. It is about allowing another person just to 'be.'

Always see if there is an 'angle' behind your actions, if there isn't then you have understood this lesson.

We are forever with you, and we are looking after you and your brother. You have connected at this time because it is important for both of your learning. There is much more ahead and either one of you can walk away at any time, but we don't want that to happen. We can see more than you both and do not have the problems you have on the Earth plain. We see your path as one and we are trying to help you both, but we can only come when you ask for help.

We have always been with you, even before you came onto your Earth walk.

Remember Sayana there is much ahead. Never lose your faith.'

The voice gradually faded away.

***

'What a wonderful dream,' Sayana yawned and stretched and stood up. 'I wonder what an Earth Plain looks like?' She mused. Somewhere in the back of her mind, she felt she knew but she could not quite recall. She walked towards the **Pool** and jumped in. She played with Grandmother Turtle, flowing through the water on her back, twisting and tumbling through the clear waters. Soon it was time to leave, and Grandmother Turtle rose to the surface and Sayana stepped onto the bank. Waiting for her were Oleron and Daath. They led the way and Sayana silently followed to the back of the **Cave**, and there in a corner were some stone steps that lead to an underground **Cavern**. As they descended, she saw a sight so overwhelming that she let out a squeal. The **Cavern** was full of jewels, glinting and glowing in the light of wall lanterns.

'Sayana these are yours. Take what you want.' Sayana looked around. Then at the back of the **Cavern** in the shadows, she saw Bear. She walked over to him and took him by the hand. She turned and said,

'You can offer me all the riches in the world, but I choose Bear. He is worth more to me than it all.'

As they turned to walk away Daath said

'Stop. You can fill your pockets and have both.'

' If we are meant to have jewels to do our work then so be it, I welcome it but together what we can create will bring the riches we need.'

They walked out of the **Cave** together and down under the willow tree and into the circle. The elders were already there, and Sayana took her place voluntarily in the centre. She faced Bear and spoke.

'I welcome change. Send me the lessons I need, so that I can grow and change. I know that sometimes the right path is not the easiest one. I have tried to own without first acknowledging love. We can always own Earth, but that is all we will ever have without love. With love, we can paint with the colours of the wind.

We speak many empty words. I must learn to speak from the heart and listen the same way. I must commit to loving and respecting myself before I can receive that from anyone else.

Chapter 14

This morning Sayana saw that she had a new Guide in her **Garden**.

'Hi, I am Finella, do you have any questions before we start?'

'Yes. Why is it that when I have a problem and I go into my sacred space to resolve it, I cannot remember what the problem was when I come back? Does that happen to everyone?'

Finella grinned at Sayana' What is the point in hanging onto things that are no longer relevant? If they have been resolved, then what do you need to remember them for?'

'Mmmm, I suppose if you put it like that I can understand. Tell me about love Finella.'

'Well help me get the room ready as we speak.'

'Do you know something I always thought this was my **Garden** and I was the only one that had access to it, so how can you lead a lecture in my **Garden**? Come to that how can I have the Living Library in the Temple of Knowledge in my **Garden**? I am sure I am not the only one to be able to access that.'

'Of course not. Everyone has the possibility to access the Library.'

'Then why don't I ever see anyone except my **Guides** and Bear, Sayana asked.

'Because you don't invite them in. Other people are also doing the same thing. They never see anyone because they don't invite them in. How many people do you see in lectures?'

'Well sometimes I see men in saffron coloured robes but usually, I'm the only one there. I thought they were only for me!'

Finella laughed. 'There are many minds there Sayana, but you cannot see a mind. This is your own private **Garden**, and you only have who you want here.'

'But how can that be? Bear came into my **Garden**, and I did not remember him. How could I want something or someone that I did not know existed?'

'Don't you remember what Bear told you "Sayana don't you know anything about your higher self? Do you know that we can all be connected somewhere outside our conscious mind?" '

'Yes, I do remember, but Finella it is very confusing.'

'Yes Sayana, no one said it was easy.'

Sayana paused thinking for a moment.

'How long do you think I will be here Finella? I begin to feel that it is soon time to leave. Is there somewhere out there, what is the Earth Plain.'

'I think it may soon be time for you to leave. You have been content just to be and learn about the **Garden**, and you have worked hard and learnt much. Outside your **Garden** is another world, another life. One day you will have the choice to go there. It is not free and flowing like it is here. There are many people out there too - lectures would indeed have to be shared! But there is a place for you there. A place for you to share your knowledge, a mission that you can choose to accept. You will know when it is time but that is not quite yet. You still have something to do in the White House, before you go.'

'Will I have to leave you, Wolf, Daath and Oleron and everyone' .... Sayana's eyes filled with tears 'and Bear.'

'Yes, I am afraid you will. But if you need us, you can call and we will come to you in Dreamtime, or in your Sacred Space.'

'I don't want to go; I want to stay here. '

'That is your choice now Sayana. But there will come a time when you must decide and only you can make that decision. Anyway, enough of this I have to prepare for the lecture, and someone is calling you, don't you hear?'

Sayana listened and she thought she heard her mother's voice, as she did on her first day in the **Garden**.' Where is she?'

'She is in the White House Sayana; it is time to go and see her.'

Finella left and Sayana turned to the Temple entrance, and walked through the doors, along the path towards the White House. She was full of apprehension. She did not want to go, there was nothing she could think of saying to her mother, but perhaps if she did not go, her mother would come to her, and she did not want that, so she walked up to the house and slowly pushed open the door.

The first thing that struck Sayana was the silence. Not a sound anywhere. She looked around. The place was spotless, and the decor was perfect. Persian rugs covered the floor, the upholstery was plush and plentiful.

'Oh, there you are. I have been calling you forever. Don't you know I need you? Your Father is busy watching football. '

Sayana looked at her mother, beautiful even in her apron. 'Why did I have to share my sacred space with someone Mum? You never explained it to me. Wasn't I good enough, is that why you needed to get me a sister? Was she better than me? You never asked me what I wanted. My hair, my clothes. I know it wasn't easy, with dad working, and then you went to work too. All you had to do was explain - you never did that. I was always different, I never felt like I belonged, except to Nan. She was my best friend. I don't blame you mum, I just wanted to understand. Will I be like this with my children? I need to understand.'

Sayana looked at her mother and she was crying; they were both crying and for the first time in her life, she and her mother hugged each other unconditionally. There was no duty, or fear of loss, there was just love.

'Your fathers in the lounge '.

She kissed her mother and walked through the door, through into the pristine cleanliness of the lounge where the TV was playing, sending out its electromagnetism into the room. Her father was watching the football, as he had always done; with his eyes closed. Sayana smiled at him in his private world and wondered what he was dreaming about. Just then he woke up and looked at her, smiled and said, 'Hello hello,' as he had always done.

'Are you busy?'

'No, just watching the football.'

'I love you Dad; we don't say that much in this family, do we?'

'No, but we all know don't we.' He gave her a wink. 'Want a cup of tea.?'

What a strange life this is she thought 'No thanks I have to be going. Just wanted to make sure you knew. Don't work so hard.' She kissed him on the 3rd wrinkle of his forehead, as she had always done and left him to his football.

Her Mother had gone when she retraced her steps. She quietly closed the door and with a sigh walked back into her **Garden**.

Chapter 15

Sayana sat on the cliff overlooking the sea and the beach far below. She felt an energy as if something was about to happen. As she watched the sky a message took shape in the clouds.

'We are interconnecting spheres of light reaching out and holding hands across the world, sharing unconditional love, ebbing and flowing.'

Then she had a Vision and knew this is what her work would be if she went back.

She saw People coming from all parts of the World. To the 'Centre of Crystal Light.' It would be a meeting place, bigger than anyone could ever imagine. People would come by ships waving as they passed. The Centre was to be a school. A place of rest. There would be an ever-flowing energy of people coming in and out. It would be a place to teach, learn and regenerate. Then she saw a white dove high in the pale blue sky with its heart-shaped wings holding a golden twelve-pointed star. She could hear singing and laughter; it would be a happy place. Then she heard a strange sound, like tinkling icicles. As she listened the words 'harmonic sound' came into her head. She had a knowing, a knowing that this sound, this toning would reach far and wide, cutting like lasers, aligning energies through sound. She knew that this sound could stop wars and heal sick bodies, and if sharp enough and in unison with others it would reach through our world and into the next. It would calm, stretching into different lands, lifting sadness, and helping the children. The compassion Sayana felt overwhelmed her then she heard a voice;

'You will teach others to heal themselves, higher than before, reaching out, back and up into the future, tuning up negative energy and turning it into positive power for healing. There will be lots of children in the centre, like a Kindergarten in some way. Parents will come to learn their jobs and you will look after the children.'

With a chuckle, the voice said' It will be a Kindergarten for all - adults and children! Your job will be to teach the children who they really are, and how to love and respect. They will then be able to help their parents and older folks.

Your position on the star is interconnecting West and East. You must bring your music to the ears of the People.

The twelve points of the star are very important. They represent Time, night and day, the Medicine wheel, the planets, the elements but most of all the four directions.

You are being given Wolf as your Guide, protector, and teacher, and together you will establish the International Light Foundation, which will help children in need around the world. There will be many hard and enlightening experiences along the way and sometimes you will want to give up because people will constantly question and try to stop the plans. But you will get stronger with every twist of fate. Do you have any questions?'

Sayana just stared into the distance.

'Sayana Listen!'

'I was, I am lost for words. I have so many questions, I do not know where to start,'

'We don't have much time, so you will need to find a place to start. Let me see.

Yes, you were born in May, which is the East, which is about hearing, so I see you were listening after all! Are you ready with your first question?

'Yes. Why me.'

'Why not! Next question'

'I don't know about children, how can I teach them, when I'm barely able to teach myself.'

'That will come. Within the next three years, many opportunities will arise for you to train but the most important lesson you will have will be where you will find tipis. This is the beginning. Here you will learn more than any teacher will ever teach you in a classroom.'

'I'm not even sure if I like children! I know I had three but that was a long time ago.'

'A child will come into your family circle that will change that. She is very special; you will learn many things from her. But look at her eyes. They will reflect the sky and lagoons and the history that has not yet begun, and the future that has long passed. She will be magical and through her, you will learn how to recognise the others. The most important action you can give the earth is to help these enlightened children to develop. They will recognise you also and tell you things that you could not share as a child. They will be like you Sayana. You are all interconnecting spheres of light on multi-dimensional levels and together you and the other enlightened ones will form a grid - a network across the world, interacting with others like yourselves, but you, through the children, can bring credibility and respect to Lightworkers by working with official agencies. There is much to learn, and it will not come at once, but it will come. This is your future unless you decide not to go back. I must go now Goodbye Sayana.'

Sayana sat for a long time on the cliff looking out across the sea.

Chapter 16

For the last time she went down to the Tipi. As she entered the flap Bear was already there waiting for her. He was drumming quietly. He smiled and gave her a wink. She suddenly realised how like her father he was. She was overwhelmed by joy but also with sorrow at the thought of the leaving which she knew in her heart would soon come.

'Bear I have something for you. I know they are words, but they come from the heart. They are my gift to you. You taught me how to live with the colours of the wind. I understand now that the wind is change, am I right?'

'Yes, Sayana you are right. I would like to hear your gift and I thank you from my heart. But first I would like to give you a gift.'

He took Sayana's hand and led her out of the Tipi to stand in front of the mighty **Waterfall**, with their back to Sacred Mountain. Wolf sat watching, content that Sayana was safe. From his pouch, Bear took a smudge stick and lit it. Very gently, he blew the smoke around her, cleansing and strengthening. She felt his breath in her aura, like a cool breeze on a warm summer day.

When he was finished, she was calmer than ever before and when she sang, the sound was like glass chimes dancing in the moonlight.

REFLECTIONS

You came to me through mists of time
a love that once was only mine.
We stand and face the shadows of our soul
we realise that when we're whole
alone we'll be within without
and never more ourselves we'll doubt.
But a question I must ask of you, Reflection dear
what's the point of being here -
if alone we'll be
just you and me?
With rainbows flowing through my mind
'Are you there,' I call, or will I find
where once Reflections glowed anew
a dimmer picture losing you.
When I'm whole, alone I'll be -
unless I know that you love me.
We travel on and learn our Quest
was to love ourselves the best.
But mirror me and we may find
an understanding that will bind
eternally and filled with joy
and life anew that we can enjoy.
Reflection please don't go away
I need you now. And each new day

a better understanding brings
of you and me and many things.
You taught me things I never knew
I never knew, I never knew
Don't go away, I've learnt so much
and in my heart the ice you touch
and as spring brings winters thaw,
I'll learn to love ME more and more.

'Don't you see? How stupid of me, of course you see!! We are reflections. You are my reflection and you played Heyoka and took me to the centre of the circle. I learnt about myself from you Bear. That is why you are in my **Garden** - you are my mirror. How painful it has been. I have learnt to love myself at last.'

They walked towards each other and held each other for a long, long time.

'Now I must go Sayana. It is time. There is nothing more I can do in your **Garden**. I love you.' He kissed her gently and she closed her eyes, merging with him, smelling the sage in his aura from the smudge. She suddenly realised that she no longer felt lonely and the feeling of homesickness was not so strong. Excitedly she opened her eyes, but he was gone. Teardrops fell from her eyes as she realised that he had walked through the **Waterfall** and back onto his Earthwalk and she may never see him again.

Chapter 17

Sayana walked into her **Garden**. She sat on her **Seat** and looked all around, at the beautiful butterflies and the rainbow-coloured flowers.

She said 'I want someone like me. Someone who I can dance and sing with. Someone I can drum the rhythm of life with. I want this dream to become reality. '

All the pain in her life she pushed away and shot a golden laser at it. As she watched it exploded and became tiny stars. They fell to the earth and as they did tiny crystals grew where they landed.

She thought hard about what she really wanted.

She wanted someone who would understand, who could dance her dance and live her life because it was theirs also. They didn't have to pretend or try because their life was already like that.

She wanted to howl with them in the moonlight. She wanted to love the children of the world and be wherever the light sent her. She wanted them to be there too, when not in body in spirit. She wanted to hold and care for them and to know that they would reflect her love because they were the same.

She stood in the middle of the grass and raised her arms to the spirit of love rooting her feet to the mother that gives earth life.

She howled, such a beautiful howl that the leaves on the willow swayed to the sound.

Wolf was watching her. He seemed to be smiling - at last, she knew what she wanted. At last, she could begin to write her book.

She thought of Bear, her brother from long ago. She called him with her mind and knew he was the same as her.

If one day they were to meet again she knew at last she could fly on the wind and he would be by her side, but if the light took them in different directions, she knew that she was at peace within and that at some time in the distant future, when this life was done they would meet again and perhaps be together next time.

At last, she was whole. She walked to the river and as she looked at her reflection she said,

'Nyah-Weh-Sgeh-noh - Thank you for being,' then she started to sing.

Oh, wey Oh wey Oh
the waters of life flowing into the soul
Oh, wey Oh wey Oh
the waters of life flowing into the soul
Mother Earth holds us close in her embrace
for many years we've lived in her breath,
the vision once was the impossible dream
now we all know what our ancestors mean
as surely as the river runs to the sea
a beautiful place for my brothers and me
oh, wey oh wey oh
the waters of life flowing into the soul
oh, wey oh wey oh
the waters of life flowing into the soul

***

It was dusk as Sayana walked back to the **Cave**, the way out of her **Garden**. It was time at last to leave.

She walked inside; the ground was cool to her feet. She heard a drum-like beat, and she edged closer to the sound, and then she heard a cry. Not from some wild beast but from her own heart. She walked through the **Cave**. Light flashed off the jewelled crystal walls. She got nearer and nearer the centre and she knew this was the closest she had ever been to her soul.

Strange music filled the air, and the sounds grew closer and closer. She knew she was nearing the end of her journey. She heard water splash a few feet away just around the rock overhang. What could the splashing be she wondered. A few more paces and she saw it, the most beautiful angel. It rose from the **Pool** just in front of her. Its wings were dripping rainbows and she watched as it rose higher and higher to the roof of the **Cave**. The angel hung in the crystal light reflecting from the **Pool**.

'Sayana - Sayana come to me, it is time.'

Sayana walked forward and stepped off the ledge. Instead of falling into the water she floated above it, higher and higher. She reached out and the magnificent angel drew her towards him. They danced in the warm summer air underneath the stars as they floated upwards far above the **Cave**.

Sayana started to sing.

'We're floating skywards in our dreams
across the celestial sky,
how much longer do we have
the world and you and I
we've been together ten thousand years,
not a day too long
but what I'd like to know right now,
is where do we all belong.

Higher and higher they floated swirling and dancing in the breeze.

Nearer and nearer to the planets they flew.

Shooting stars and galaxies called to them through the night sky. Home, home at last they headed.

Then Sayana remembered her mission, the one she had talked to Daath about, the one she had written in her book. She stopped dancing and with tears in her eyes she said,

'Go. I cannot come home yet; my mission is not yet finished. Thank you for coming for me but I have made my decision - I must go back.'

She reached out and touched the angel's wings then let go.

Chapter 18

Sayana was stirring, just coming back from Dreamtime. The surroundings looked oddly familiar although she felt like it had been years since she was here. Gradually she recognised that she was in a hospital ward and the flowers and cards gave her a warm glow. She felt different, at peace within herself. An independence radiated throughout her being, soft and gentle.

She heard a familiar laugh outside and the door opened.

'Hello, how are you today? I hear you've been very sick.'

'Yes, I think I have,'

'I missed you at the drumming workshop last week and when I asked around, someone told me you were in here. Then I had a dream about you last night. So, I thought I'd come and see you, see if you need anything.'

He made himself comfortable by the bed and handed her a single red rose.

'I took the thorns off, didn't want you hurting yourself.' He laughed a tender caring laugh.

'Thanks, it's good to see you. Tell me what the dream was about.'

'Well, it was strange really, I know you like to sing but I saw you in the middle of a **Garden** looking radiant and howling like a wolf and I was sitting near you drumming. '

Suddenly for the first time in her life, Sayana didn't feel homesick.

She looked at this ruggedly handsome man, a red man in a white body and she knew they were the same, she also knew she'd made the right decision.

Her life was about to begin again, but this time she would not be alone.

She smiled and he winked –

just as they had always done.

REFLECTIONS

NOTES ON THE SYMBOLOGY OF THE JOURNEY

Authors Note

When I wrote this book in the mid 1990's there was no Google to help me as that wasn't available to the public until 2004 so I was not influenced as to what I found in my **Garden**: the characters, the buildings, or the idea. It came directly as a result of my NDE in 1991 and my subsequent meditations. That in itself was an adventure. To help me recover from my illness which was a result of salmonella poisoning in 1991, my daughter Wendy paid for me to go on holiday. I went to the Sahara desert and met a spiritual master who taught me how to meditate. It was after this that **Secret Garden** continued to come to me through my meditations.

Therefore knowledge in this book was not the result of a research project but actual events.

Editing this book in 2023 for publishing has led me to delve into the meaning of some of the things I found in my **Garden** and to clarify what I have believed all these years. My research came up with some rather interesting information which I thought I would share, so I have added some notes. But don't forget this is my **Garden,** not yours, so you may never find what I have found, in your own **Garden**. Although over the thousands of people that I have taught this to, there are some definite similarities. This to me shows that we are all connected in some way, even to the placing of certain objects in our **Gardens**.

Politically Correct Terminology

I do not wish to cause any controversy with my references to Native, Native American, or African people, but this book was written 30 years ago when most people had not encountered the use of politically correct terminology!

I have thought long and hard about the words in this book as I edit this manuscript and although I have removed some of chapter 12 and 13, I have decided to leave the rest of The Journey as I originally wrote it. I didn't want to change too much because I wanted it to be true to what actually happened, and although it might read like it, it isn't fiction - it is an experience that I had.

I apologise if it upsets the reader

If you would like to read the unabridged version of chapters 12 & 13 please get in touch at www.TriciaFrances.co.uk

REFLECTIONS
NOTES ON THE SYMBOLOGY OF THE JOURNEY

Some of the events in the story happened in October 1991 when I arrived at the hospital. I was admitted to a single room as they were not sure if what I had was contagious. Turned out to be Salmonella. The rest of the events happened during the following 2 or 3 years when I was discovering my own **Secret Garden**. However, my **Garden** continued to grow long after that time.

Sayana. This character is me. In the following notes, I have referred to Sayana in the third person to avoid confusion with the story and the present. I was given the name Sayana Wolf by native people when I ran a charity project for them, which became known as Sayana Wolf Trust. Wolf was our mascot for the project. See **Wolf**

Chapter 1

NDE – Near Death Experience

Synchronicity - The occurrence of meaningful coincidences that seem to have no cause.

Wolf is my Animal Guide. He is the teacher and protector of children. Before I knew about that, I was given the name of Sayana Wolf – Teacher of the Children - after being involved with Native Americans and running education and charity projects with them in the late

90's (see my autobiography for more information on this project). I went on to found a children's charity, led afterschool and holiday clubs, and became an Art teacher for 15 years for all age groups but mainly high school, where I saw first-hand how Art can help to build strong creative young people.

Daath is Knowledge on a soul level. My research pulled up the GLORIAN which explains more about Daath, which in many ways fits into my book, but my Daath was a Guide, a being in my **Garden**. There is a doorway and a tree as described in the Glorian. Perhaps during my NDE, I tapped into that consciousness.

Red Roses. To this day, over 30 years later coloured flowers do not grow in my physical **Garden**! Except for my pink buddleia and beautiful pink and white Japanese Flamingo Willow (Salix Integra Hakuro Nishiki). I can't even grow a red rose. The colour in my **Garden** comes from the trees and bushes – every shade of green.

Chapter 2

Clackers were a toy of the 60's and 70's. They consisted of a string with a glass ball on each end. The object was to hold the string in the centre and move your hand up and down so that the balls swung and clacked together, ultimately getting them to swing high enough to clack at the top as well as the bottom. I was good at this! They were dangerous and later banned, and a plastic substitute was introduced.

The Red Rubber Sports Floor. In the mid 90's whilst running the Light Foundation – the charity which I founded – we were on the verge of getting a huge lottery grant and were negotiating for large empty premises with land to use as the charity headquarters. I looked in the buildings for one that could be used as a convention centre and found the sports hall. There was the red rubber floor, just as I had seen in my NDE. I knew this was the place we had been searching for. But the local councils couldn't agree on who owned it, so we lost the Lottery grant. I later realised how that place would have distracted me from focusing on our work and just like my story, I would have become manipulated by rules and regs and answering to others. It turned out to be a positive warning.

The Old Lady. 30 years on – that old woman with white hair is me now! Walking with one foot on the road and one foot on the gutter has led to needing a stick (although I don't use it – would probably trip myself up with it!) How could I have described myself so well all those years ago?

Chapter 3

This was the first trip to the **Temple of Knowledge** where all the books of every life that ever existed on this planet are stored; the Akashic records, otherwise known as the Living Library. Perhaps the records stretch further than this planet, I don't know the answer to that, but it is truly a great place. It is a place to learn.

Since I first saw it in my meditations I have seen images of it online and in movies like Harry Potter, so no doubt other writers and photographers have resonated with that place. What an amazing feeling it is to be watching a film and suddenly recognise the place which I have known for many years in my **Secret Garden**!

The Hall of Bodies is where the blueprints are stored in the form of a body at the time of our spiritual awakening. Before we get here to the Earth plain we work out what we have to learn this time, and this determines the age, gender, and type of body we need to achieve those lessons – hence the selection of bodies.

Boats represent ideas and opportunities. Many of those come from visiting the Temple. *On the water in front of the Temple of Knowledge.*

I know now that was the upcoming work with children which at that point I had no idea at all that was where my future was heading. I was an entertainer at the time when everything changed! (NDE1991). If they are broken and wrecked it is a sign that you are not making the most of them or you have missed them along the way.

Temple Guides are brown-robed hooded figures that help to deliver lessons in the Temple.

Chapter 4

Cave. Interestingly my **Cave** moved to another location after a while, and stayed there, which is the location I have used in The Workbook and Study Guide. Its original location served to be too complicated to get to when teaching **Secret Garden**, and it moved automatically. If your **Cave** is in a different place, then that's where it's meant to be for you – at least at the beginning! But the Waterfall and Cave are the entrance to your Garden.

Jumping the Void. *DO NOT TRY THIS IN THE PHYSICAL*! It is an exhilarating thing when done in meditation. It can break down barriers and give a sense of freedom. Sometimes in our lives, we are standing on the edge of something great. We can either stay where we are wondering what would have happened or take a leap of faith and trust that it will work out. In this case, the bird caught Sayana and flew her to safety on the beach. Everything is how it is meant to be.

Osiris (otherwise known as Osirus). One of my main **Guides** in The Journey. My research shows that this Guide was an Egyptian God who ruled humanely, teaching elements of civilization. He travelled the world conquering and teaching men, by wisdom not war, as he had in Egypt. But his jealous brother Set killed him and Osiris became God of the afterlife, the dead, resurrection, and life which seems fitting as I am having an NDE at the time!

The Sacred Mountain. The journey up the mountain was about being resourceful and overcoming my fears.

Ridicule when you speak your truth. In 1990's that happened when I tried to share what I found in my meditations! When I talked about the planet, what we needed to do, climate changes and many other things, mostly people didn't listen and thought I had cracked! Those people gradually drifted away, and I met people of the same mind. Now in 2023, most people have some idea of what we need to do to save the planet, the creatures, and ultimately, the People.

The Great White Spirit helps us with our Awakening.

When the Wind Blows you Bend but when the Hurricane comes you stand strong. This is something that came to me right at the beginning. In life, we have many small situations to deal with where we have to bend a bit to compromise for a happy ending for all. Other times things become much more difficult, and we have to stand our ground. Those are the Hurricanes!

The following 3 are connected.

Aloneness v Loneliness. *I expect everyone feels a sense of loneliness at some point in their lives, which is quite different to Aloneness. Loneliness is an emotional feeling that something is missing. Aloneness is a state of being knowing you don't need anyone else to be complete.*

Homesick. Like that feeling you have when you are away on holiday and all you can think about is getting home because you miss it your home comforts or the people there. But this doesn't relate to those things. It's just a feeling like something is missing that you have never been able to find. What you have been looking for all this time is right there – it's you!

Super People. *These are people that are strong in themselves but form relationships with others like themselves. The relationships of the future on Earth.*

When I wrote that 30 years ago I had no idea what that was to become, but I imagined the masculine and feminine sides of our personalities would lose the hard edges and become softer and more interwoven. Over the years I have seen many of those types of relationships grow. Where people are strong and stronger together. Although there are still some unequal partnerships, I have seen an increase in younger people who are supportive equally with each other. The kind of relationships that older people could only dream of in the past.

Chapter 5

The View reminds us to look at situations from a higher level. See L'Oriel.

The Ravine, the Sacrifice & the Shrunken Heads. The story tells of a fear of carved masks and idols and how they were pushed into the ravine. The ravine represents a deep fear whether from this or past lives. It is true that I have always found those statues and masks very unsettling in the past. They do not bother me now, although I would rather not have them in my house!

Chapter 6

The Wind of Change. Remember the affirmation 'when the wind blows you bend but when the hurricane comes stand strong'? Change can be very powerful and difficult for some people or situations. We can crumble and cry but in the end we have to deal with situations life throws at us. By thinking and deciding on what we want or don't want in our lives we make the first steps to changing it. See **Thought Creates!** above.

Thought Creates! Because it does! This has been my affirmation for many years. Think about it. Nothing could have been invented or experienced without thought. Even if something happens in your life that is an utter surprise or seemingly out of your control it could only have happened because of a thought by you – or someone else. The house you live in – builder or designer thought about how it would look. The car you drive, someone thought up the design. The clothes you wear again a thought created the design and you thought it would look good on you. So what about negative thought? Think of the positive effect they have had / or will have on your life?

The question is where did the first thought come from that created the Earth? That's a whole other discussion!

Chapter 7

The Fear of Being Alone. *'Aloneness is not the same thing as Loneliness.'* This was a powerful realisation because that fear of being alone created loneliness. It's coming to terms with being comfortable when you are on your own, that changes everything. (See chap 4)

Chapter 8

12 years to put it right. Back then in 1995, when I first wrote this part of my book, we seemed to be on the edge of something apocalyptic. There was an urgency that the world would change, and we had 12 years to prepare as the end was nigh! And it happened, not in the way that could be foreseen but catastrophic just the same! 2007 was the age of technology – internet evolved, and social media took off. Life would never be the same again. It is not all bad though. There are many positive things about technology which have evolved since 2007. But have we come to rely on it a bit too much?

You can't help but love how synchronicity works. Whilst writing this reflection chapter an electrician came to my house to do a repair and in conversation he mentioned that the iPhone was introduced in 2007, which of course played a major part of the changes at that time and since. I did not know that previously, but now that adds weight to the events of 2007.

The 3 Nomads. The story initially shows how we get clues in our lives about how to deal with things, but it's up to us to 'write' our own version of the story. Each person's story and search for their Holy Grail will be different – but ultimately it is about finding and loving yourself.

Daath describes himself in more detail here. *Some people call me Death. I am the bringer of souls.* He explains that there is no death just a transition from physical body to the next incarnation and that the spirit does not die. He is *The Light* through which all creation occurs seen either as the Tree of Life or a Doorway. I found that doorway on top of my mountain. I had to make the choice whether to go through it back into my life – although it won't ever be the same again - or stay in Dreamtime and move on to the next incarnation.

Oleron is the next guide. He seems angelic. I have been able to find nothing out about him in my research for this book.

The Creators Original Vision. Like any project or organisation on a large or small scale, the original plan will change over time. Imagine the creation of Earth as a project. The original intention is for the good with positive outcomes. Then some of the employees, or project managers see a different way to proceed, and their plan either goes wrong or becomes about greed and manipulation. They will either get fired or gain enough support that the original vision fades into the background.

Great Creator and Mother Earth that will restore the balance. Well certainly that is happening! The number of natural disasters is increasing by the day. Perhaps climate change is part of the bigger picture to bring us back to the original vision.

L'Oriel '*The projecting window of upper storey*' - meaning a higher view. See **The View**

Something from Nothing & the Void. Imagine the Void, a place where there is nothing. You enter and immediately that place now has something.

The Blanket. So the wind of change took everything away, and the only thing that was needed right then was the blanket for warmth and comfort given by a friend. When we think we have lost everything, there will be someone there to help us with what we really need right then.

Chapter 9

The Garden. We don't always take the time to get into nature, whether it's in our own **Garden**, or a walk in the park or buy the sea. Listening to the birds, or the wind in the trees or watching the ripples in the river its part of life. I remember teaching in urban schools where many children sat indoors playing on their Video Games Consoles at every opportunity. Some children said they didn't like being in natural surroundings. It's amazing that they felt like that against the very thing needed to keeps them alive!

Blank spaces or voids in the **Garden** are areas which you have not yet explored.

Barriers, Walls & Fences in your **Secret Garden** refer to barriers in life. Things that need to be changed to give a clear unobstructed view. It's better to change things with love which creates a better outcome.

Treasures in the Dross. Sometimes we miss special things in life because they don't come in nice, neat packages and seem like rubbish or a waste of time. You know when you are struggling, and someone offers you advice, but you don't listen because it seems like nonsense. Perhaps in that offer there could be a treasure which you have yet to find. *The problems in life bring forth the greatest gifts.*

The Documents from the leather bag. Even now after all this time there are still areas which could use improvement!! Particularly *#3* ***How to Win****. Eat sleep and work to proportion, never be in 'Want.'* I still work too many hours without enough sleep!

Have what you need. Move any surplus around so that it gets used beneficially. Holding on causes blocks. This is a constant issue in my life but now I have retired from my commercial art & craft work this is getting better.

We can't do everything at once – whether on the physical, mental, or emotional level, there is always something to work on. Mine is to work on getting more sleep and having less clutter!

Chapter 10

Write That Book. Well I finally am writing that book. It mentions this phrase a few times in the chapter which I had completely forgotten was in there. Going back 3 years prior to the publication of this book, I saw a popup for a writing course which focused on how to get your book over the line. As it had been nearly 30 years since I last published my books I thought it would be invaluable for me to see how publishing had moved on. And I am so glad I did that pop up because I went on to do 3 x **Write That Book** masterclasses with author Michael Heppell. It resulted in the writing and publishing of my Autobiography in 2022. Then when editing this book for publication in 2023, I was stunned to see that phrase. Synchronicity strikes again!

It says in the Journey that when I write this book I will be writing my future and that I will have got to a point in this incarnation where I will have freedom and control. The book is about my growing. Well in December 2022 I retired from my art & craft business. So perhaps that is what was meant by freedom, I certainly have more of that. If I am writing my future then I look forward to what comes next because much of this book has already become reality!

White Buffalo a sacred animal guide.

Sarah. Purple robed Guide gives Sayana the keys to the Temple of Knowledge.

The Crystal Summer House. The **Inner Sanctuary** and you will find a Meditation in the Workbook, but it shows you how to access it from the **Cave** not the **Garden**.

Karma is a physical action, the law of cause and effect, or ethical causation. To be mindful of what do can create positive Karma. Some karmic payback is instant – some takes a long time – perhaps even more than one life. The chapter in The Journey describes it fully. I wrote this section of the chapter in 1995 and a few years later it was published in a few magazines including Eastern Light and Rainbow Bridge.

Walking in Nature. This is something we often neglect in our 21st century life.

The Game of Love is often dangerous as the dance of the Scorpion and the Mantis showed.

Chapter 11

The Sun Dial is the natural clock, showing real-time by the sun. Invented over 3500 years ago by the Egyptians. In this case the Sun Dial related to learning on her Journey.

Other people's journeys. We no doubt influence people on our journey through life, by just being there but we should not have access to their life book – that is private to them.

Chapter 12

Earth Walk. This life/incarnation on the Earth.

White Bear. There are references in this chapter to Sayana's Native American brother. Whilst editing this book I researched this name, and it appears that he was a Kiowa Chief named Satanta who lived in the 1800's. For the purposes of this book, I have just called him Bear.

Chapter 13

The Mountain – overcoming obstacles and fears. Note it was much easier for Sayana to reach the mountain this time than it was in Chapter 4.

The Circle – Life & Connection. The energy created in a circle is very powerful and often used as a metaphor for gaining spiritual knowledge in a group situation i.e. joining a circle. You can finish something by working through it back to the beginning.

12 Elders – these wise people are **Guides** and are there to help Sayana see what needs to be worked on.
The Crystal. See Chapter 10 in the Workbook for this meditation.

Grandmother Turtle. A wise guide which teaches us about Truth and Life.

Cavern was full of jewels. This abundance could be an illusion. Sayana looked deep into this secret part of her **Cave** and saw Bear which she recognised as more valuable to her than the crystals. She could have had both but decided not to be tempted.

Chapter 14

Finella. Another Guide

Problems. Once we resolve a problem let it go, it is no longer of any use.

The White House. This represents the Family. Sayana was apprehensive of entering but she was able to connect at last with her mother unconditionally and with her father in an easy loving way – as she had always done.

Chapter 15

This Vision led to the founding of The Light Foundation charity and Projects. It's a long story and best read about in my autobiography 'It's All About Me! & William the Conqueror's Grandfather.

Tipis. I visited a Tipi village on a mountain top in Spain where I learnt about the Talking stick during a circle gathering, where those holding the stick had the floor to speak uninterrupted. A week later I started a new career as an after-school and holiday club leader and during a meeting of Club Leaders and Children's services, I introduced them to the Talking Stick, which was adopted by many of the Out of School Clubs. It happened within 3 years of my NDE!

Teaching. A few years later I did indeed become a teacher.

The very special Child did come into my family circle, and she changed everything for which I am eternally thankful. X

Lightworkers are *interconnecting spheres of light on multi-dimensional levels sharing unconditional love.* Lightworking was my work for many years travelling around the world. Now I am older I am trusting that this book will continue to do that work for years to come.

Chapter 16

Smudge. See Notes for chapters 3 & 4 in Study Guide

Heyoka is the sacred clown, the trickster, an empath, a healer, and contrarian. Bear is a Heyoka on some levels that help Sayana.

Reflections. Other people can be reflections of us, and from them, we can learn about ourselves.

Wind of change – see Chapter 6 above.

Earthwalk. In this situation, this refers to Bear returning to his current life on Earth.

Chapter 17

Nyah-Weh-Sgeh-noh - Thank you for being. A Seneca greeting.

Angel – this could be Oleron. See Chapter 8. It came for Sayana but as she was leaving she realised that she had to come back to complete her mission on Earth.

Chapter 18

Back to Life. Sayana leaves Dreamtime and her NDE and I return to my life which at that time is in the hospital.

Bear. He did come into my life – twice. We had fun, and we learned from each other but this time we were not ready – maybe next life!

Afterword

Well, I finally wrote it, only took 30 years! Having a tool like **Secret Garden** that I could use in my own way when I need it, I found really useful over the years.

I hope that you have gained something from my book and found out a bit more about You. Even if you just learned how to relax, then it did its job.

Thank you for reading.
Tricia x

ACKNOWLEDGEMENTS

I would like to thank my **Secret Gardener** Beta Readers for seeing if it worked on paper.

My Alpha Readers Monica and Liam for their great editorial feedback.

Matt Bird for typesetting.

Jenny, Art & Sales Coordinator from Magic Eye Inc for her help.

And Cassie for her love and support to keep me and my house going whilst my head was in my book!

About the Author

Born in London in the 1950's, I found my true home when I came to Norfolk on holiday in the early 1980's and didn't go home!

I have been a Writer and Artist for more than 50 years. I wrote my first memoir aged 15 knowing that I would write my autobiography when I retired. Both happened in 2022. **'It's All About Me! & William the Conqueror's Grandfather'** also led me to research my ancestors - the deGray family.

In the 1990's I wrote articles and reviews for various magazines and local papers and had my Poetry, Aromatherapy and Vegan Cook Books published. They were reprinted in 2023.

In 1991 during a Near Death Experience through food poisoning, I had a vision which resulted in the beginnings of **Secret Garden.** The technique progressed when I went to the Sahara desert and met a Spiritual Master who taught me how to meditate. (That's what I call falling down a hole and finding a ladder!) After a few years of developing it, I started to teach **Secret Garden** across the UK and later Europe.

I had taken Foundation Art at college in the 1970's and 30 years later I went on to take counselling and psychology qualifications, and BA, BSc, and Master in Education degrees.

This led to an opportunity to teach Art & Textiles in high school which I loved.

I am so fortunate to have always worked in the creative arts as both an Author and Artist.

Now that I am retired from teaching I write downstairs in my office and create art upstairs in my studio - the perfect combination!

Secret Garden has been with me for over 30 years, and I am happy that I can finally share it with more people through my book.

References

https://www.regain.us/advice/love/whats-the-idea-behind-if-you-love-something-set-it-free/

https://www.hayhouse.co.uk/heal-your-body

https://en.wikipedia.org/wiki/Smudging

https://www.magiceye.com/faq-items/help-how-do-i-see-in-3d/
https://senecalanguage.com/

https://accessgenealogy.com/montana/kiowa-tribe.htm

You can contact me through my websites or Facebook.

www.TriciaFrances.co.uk or www.TriciaFrances-deGray.co.uk where you can find my autobiography and my work with my Ancestors.

https://www.facebook.com/SecretGarden.TriciaFrances

Other publications by Tricia Frances

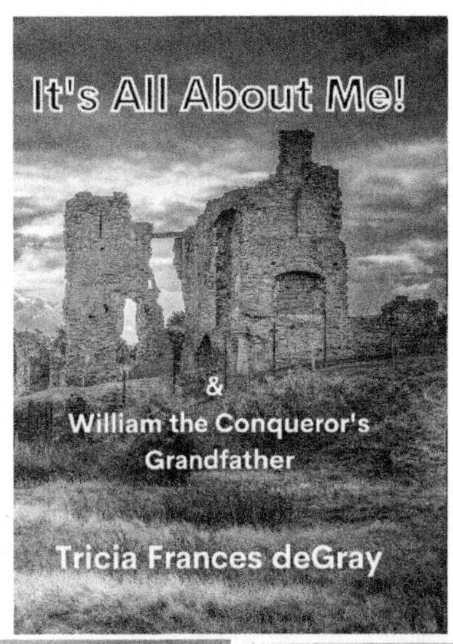

Available from https://www.triciafrances.co.uk/books

Printed in Great Britain
by Amazon